Have Gravel, will Travel

The official Tommy Bruce Biography

by Dave Lodge

Have Gravel, will Travel

The official Tommy Bruce Biography

by Dave Lodge

Pixeltweaks
PUBLICATIONS

Published in 2015
© Copyright Dave Lodge

ISBN: 978-0-992751-48-7

Updated version of the 2006 edition
(ISBN: 978-1-904502-92-0)

Cover design and book interior update by Russell Holden
www.pixeltweakspublications.com

Pixel❋tweaks
PUBLICATIONS

Acknowledgements

My thanks go to Tommy, his wife Ida and their family, Peter and Linda Leonard, Dave Chevron, Mighty Mac McGinty, Hal Carter, Mac Poole and all the people who have supported Tommy along the way.

My apologies to those people who have helped Tommy and been part of certain times in his life who have not been mentioned.

While every effort has been made to establish the rights of people to the photographs used after a period of more than forty-five years this has proved difficult if not impossible. People who I can credit are Larry Barton and the late Pat and Ken Hellier, also Rod and Nora Dolman.

Had it not been for the inspiration given to me by Roger Arthur I may never have even started this book let alone finished it so my thanks go to you. Thank you Roger.

In the course of writing this, my sole intent has been to record as accurately as possible Tommy's life with no intended offence to any person living or dead. I have tried to remain true to everything he has told me. I hope I have succeeded.

This book is dedicated to my wife Margaret with my love and gratitude for her support in all I do.

I also dedicate it to our much-loved friend Danny Williams who passed away whilst I was writing this book.

Always in our hearts Danny we know you will be waiting round the bend.

Contents

Foreword

When Dave told me he was going to try and write about my life I was surprised although a little flattered. After we had talked for a while I realized that Dave really thought that I had an interesting story to tell.

As time has gone by and I have been having my own problems with illness, hopefully now resolved, I was surprised even though I know what a hard worker and a thinker Dave is, by the diligence he applied to the task. When he brought me a synopsis of the book and read it to me while I was ill, I was amazed by what he had written because it showed that on all the long journeys we have made in the car he was listening to every word I said. I was fascinated to hear my own childhood experiences and everything that has happened in my life so far, related to me.

I know he has written this book with attention to detail and the affection shared between us seems very clear to me. What more can I say about this man who was a fan, who became my friend, my manager, without a contract I might add, and can only be described as the brother I would have wished for. I always sleep easy in my bed knowing that Dave is around taking care of business no matter what happens.

Thanks for this book bruvver.

Tommy Bruce
Entertainer and Columbia recording artiste

Sadly in 2006, not long after the first edition of this book was published, Tommy passed away. The decision was made to keep the book as it was written back then as a tribute to Tommy, including the many letters of support and well wishes received from friends 'in the business' when the book was originally published. In the years since then there are a few more that have joined Tommy in the dance hall in the sky... hopefully they ain't misbehavin!

It's early 1960 as I recall I am living with my future wife in Notting Hill Gate. Renting her basement flat is the man who changed my life. The first time I met him he was washing his car. Good-looking boy, great blonde barnet, twinkling blue eyes and built like a middleweight boxer.

I said to him "you should be a pop singer, can you sing?" he looked at me shrugged and said, " I don't know I've never tried," so I said, "let's make a demo," and we did.

At that time I was singing at The Mandrake Jazz Club with The Tony Ross Trio so I decided to use them for the session. I found a cheap studio, I think it cost me in total about £7.00! We used a song that I thought just might be a hit again "Ain't Misbehavin".

When the band and I heard Tom's voice I knew we had something - an original sound and that is perhaps the most important ingredient in pop music. We agreed I would be Tom's manager and I took the demo (an acetate which after about ten plays would wear out) to the legendary Norrie Paramour at EMI on Great Castle Street. He smiled when he heard it, then sat down at the piano in his office, played the great old tune and mused, "it might just work as a Cha Cha".

The rest is history, Tommy stormed the charts, we were in the music business and I had taken my first step towards becoming a songwriter. I owe all that has happened since to one of the nicest guys I have ever met, "The Blonde Bombshell" of song who took the UK music business by storm all those years ago Tommy Bruce.

Barry Mason
International award winning songwriter.

Chapter One

On July 16th 1937 the first raucous cries of someone who would become a star of British popular music were heard, this child would grow up to be the great rock and roller, and all round entertainer Tommy Bruce. His voice would be so powerful and so different, as to defy description, the word novelty would be used but time would prove he would be so much more than that. Now we will share with him a great journey, a journey along what has to be described as the gravel road, because of his distinctive, if not to say unique voice, which has been the key to his success in the entertainment business.

Thomas Charles[*] and his twin sister Helen were born to poor but loving parents Joseph Ambrose Bruce and Rose Violet Bruce; they already had two daughters, Rose and Constance. In these austere days Joe and Rose were living through the depression that blighted the life of many families in the thirties. Tommy's father was fortunate enough in those times of high unemployment to have a job. He was employed as a dust inspector at the corporation tip, this in simple terms meant he sorted out non-

* Tommy's full name is Thomas Charles Joseph Bruce

perishable items from the general rubbish for separate disposal. He also found that he was able to earn extra money at the then famous Bill Klein's Gym by using a skill he possessed in his hands, to give rub downs and massages to top fighters of the day such as Joe Baskey, Freddie Mills and Bruce Woodcock. He used to take Tommy along with him and whilst there, took the opportunity to give him a bit of coaching in the noble art along the lines of keep your guard up and your chin down, a bit of foot work to improve his balance, that sort of thing, for the purpose of rudimentary self-defence. As a young lad growing up in the East End of London at that time, it paid to be a bit handy and have the ability to look after yourself. This was something Tommy would have reason to be grateful for not too much later in his life.

The family lived on the Mile End road, so Tommy really was born within the sound of Bow Bells. Unlike many who style themselves cockneys, Tommy is the real deal. That is why he likes the comedy *Only Fools and Horses*. He grew up knowing guys like Del Boy and as he says might well have been a bit of a wide boy himself if it had not been for a couple of dramatic changes of direction in his life.

However, not too much later the family moved to Camden Town to live in the idyllically named property, the Doll's House so named for its size. However life for the Bruce family was far from idyllic, these were difficult days with not a lot of opportunity for anybody to improve their standard of living. Although they loved their children dearly, life was hard and it was difficult to find enough work to provide for them.

It would be easy for people these days to say you shouldn't have children if you can't afford them. But in the thirties knowledge of contraception among the working class was sketchy to say the least and large families were quite a normal thing. Life was very different then.

As pleased as their parents were to have two healthy babies when Tommy and twin sister Helen were born, it soon became apparent that they could not afford to care properly for both the new babies as well as Connie and Rose. So the hard decision had to be made that one of the twins would have to be adopted, albeit within the family. This was heartbreaking but Tommy's parents were sure that it would be best to allow childless relations, Uncle Henry and his wife to adopt Helen. This was a decision taken for the benefit of all the children, one that, in these times may seem hard to understand, but in those austere and difficult days of the Thirties many families were faced with these circumstances.

Putting this behind them, although staying in touch with Helen and her new parents, the Bruce family moved on again to Prebend Place. Actually this arrangement would mean that Helen would have a happy and settled family life, unlike the other children who had some terrible shocks in store for them. Prebend Place would be where, in time, youngest sister Shirley was born and where Tommy would start his schooldays at Richard Cobden Primary. A likeable and mischievous boy he made friends easily and entered fully into school life.

Tommy with his 'barra' at Covent Garden Market

The proud owner of his first car

Connie & Rosie, Tommy's sisters

Knowing Tommy for many years brings to mind an extremely talented performer. With not only a great talent as an actor and "Major Recording Star" but also that certain warmth which an actor or performer of any type simply must have for television, film and theatre audiences to appreciate and enjoy.

Tommy has worked with me on several of my television shows giving not only performances of the highest standard, but also a warmth that flows through the television screen to viewers that shows star quality. However more important than that is the fact that he is a "Great Guy".

Ernest Maxin
Television Producer/Director.

Writing any foreword can be a thoughtful experience. Writing one for someone like Tommy Bruce is not only thoughtful but also really surprising. Surprising because those people who remember his recording, Stage and Television appearances may not know the unusual way these things came about.

I am sure the readers of this book will be amazed at how it all began for Tommy. I would not like to spoil the surprises that are waiting for them, I'll just say that it is quite a story and an exciting one too.

It is the sort of thing that perhaps could not happen today, but back in the days when Tommy began his career, there were people in show business circles who had a feeling for talent when it might not have been apparent to others.

Luckily a certain person, one Barry Mason, who met Tommy when he was doing an ordinary job, cleaning his car I believe and amusing himself by singing a song or two he'd heard on the radio. The rest is show business history.

Enjoy the book I am sure that when you have read it you will feel you were part of Tommy's show business journey.

Bill Pertwee
Actor and Best Selling Author

What can I say about Tommy Bruce! I've only known him but a few short years, we first met when his manager Dave Lodge said Tommy would come along to appear on one of my charity shows in Doncaster, along with Craig Douglas, Jimmy Cricket and the Grumbleweeds.

Now the worst spot on any show, is to try and follow the Weeds when they have just done a 'stormer' and not only that, but to go on at 11.15pm to a rowdy audience, but! Tommy was totally unfazed, he went out there and just did the business! And I just stood and watched him and thought 'this guy is a true pro!'

I'm pleased to say we've been friends ever since and I've made several suits and shirts for both Tommy and Dave, and they in turn have helped me to raise cash for handicapped children, so I was really saddened when I heard that Tommy was suffering from the big 'C' but equally as thrilled when Dave rang me to say that they just heard that he was to be given the 'all clear'.

But I can't close without mentioning one thing '*showbiz would be a better place if all acts had a manager like Dave Lodge,*'

Neil Crossland
Stagewear Unlimited

Chapter Two

Tommy showed an early sign of the entertainer he would become when he won a children's talent show singing '*Sarah Sarah Sitting In The Shoe Shine Shop*', wearing a top hat and looking every inch The Artful Dodger. As he recalls it was the mistakes he made that had the audience in fits of laughter that helped him to win the prize.

The 5/- prize was much appreciated as young Tommy was already showing a good degree of business acumen. He was always full of ideas and schemes to make a penny here and there. Although it has to be said, some of his schemes would get him into the most awful scrapes.

One such scrape was with his sister Rose. Times were hard and winters cold and the lack of a fire prompted the children to think of stealing some fuel. It was decided between them that they should go for coal with one of the wheelbarrows that their father used to hire out to anyone who had items to move, in an effort to raise extra cash.

Heading off to the coal yard on Fire Engine Hill, so named for its close proximity to the Fire Station, both filled with enthusiasm for the task ahead. They thought they had the ideal plan and would soon be home with a full wheelbarrow. Unfortunately the plan did not work too well as Tom slipped down the coal chute, landing in the coal yard in front of the foreman and his men. They might have been prosecuted but for Tom's mournful face causing the men to take pity on them saying to the foreman; "he's only a kid, give them a chance, let them go". Eventually the foreman, after much pleading from the men and more mournful looks from Tom, relented and, giving them a good telling off, let them go home.

Tommy and Rose raced home forgetting all about the wheelbarrow, only to be faced with their father saying; "that's good, someone's hired a barrow, who was it?" The children remained silent and offered no explanation. Their father was puzzled as to the whereabouts of the barrow, but in the absence of any reason being given for its disappearance, he spent the rest of his life thinking it had been stolen by a passer-by.

One of Tommy's enterprising schemes involved taking a walk up the canal, passed the Idris factory to Camden Market. Once there he would look around the fruit stall for damaged fruit, bruised or otherwise imperfect. These were known as 'specs' and he would take them home and cut out the damaged area. Then he would put them in a box, stand on a street corner at lunchtime and sell them to passers-by for a penny. This desire to make pennies would save Tommy's life, in the very near future.

One favourite pastime of the local children was to swim in the canal during the warm weather. One day during the summer holidays one of Tommy's pals, Ernie Green, was hanging around with him and Tommy asked him to go up to Camden Market and collect some 'specs', Ernie said he'd rather go swimming. After some time, with the boys arguing back and forth, they couldn't agree on what they should do, so both went their separate ways. Tommy went up to Camden Market and Ernie set off to go swimming.

On his return journey Tommy found a crowd on the canal bank. He asked what was happening only to be told that young Tommy Bruce and Ernie Green were missing feared drowned. Tommy's father was in the canal with other men searching desperately for his son and Ernie. Ernie sadly was found trapped under the bank, it was too late to save him. Tommy thinks of him often, even now after more than sixty years.

Needless to say the sight of Tommy, fit and well on the bank, was one of the happiest moments of his dad's life. The relief in his face and the warmth and power of his embrace left Tommy in no doubt of his father's love and affection for him. Of course there was great sadness in the community at having lost Ernie so young. But that was tempered by the fact that two boys could have been lost, and while Ernie's family would never get over their loss, other people were living in hard times and so had to put it all behind them and got on with their lives.

In Norrie's office

As some one who has a great tradition of seeing the best in Rock and Roll. I saw Bill Haley at the Dominion Theatre Totenham court Road; I saw Jerry Lee Lewis and Buddy Holly when they first appeared in this country in the late fifties. I know a great rock and roller when I hear one and Tommy Bruce is right up there with the best.

I was privileged to meet Tommy for the first time when he came along to a Heritage lunch to honour Billy Fury. In fact he was part of the team who unveiled the Blue Plaque prior to the lunch. I found him to be a quiet unassuming man who gave no hint of the posturing and preening very often associated with some artistes who achieved so much in show business. He appears to have remained the same person who worked in Covent Garden market all those years ago, in spite of achieving great success in his chosen field of entertainment.

Tommy Bruce and his manager Dave Lodge the author of this book have been welcome additions to the Heritage team and all of us involved look forward to spending many more years in their company. I personally look forward to getting to know him better and strengthening our friendship.

David Graham.
Chairman of The Heritage Foundation.

Tommy Bruce was one of the top chart performers on the Rock and Trad show that I toured with. He had already had a massive hit with *'Ain't Misbehavin'* and was very popular with the audiences. I was there not just as one of the Vernon Girls, I was also one of the solo acts and Tommy and I used to do a duo spot together on the show.

These duo spots used to involve wearing silly costumes and sometimes I found them quite embarrassing. However Jack Goode and Larry Parnes always got their way about show content so there was not much point in arguing.

One particular outfit I had to wear was Tiger skin and I felt really embarrassed and silly running about the stage with the long tail trailing out behind. The guys in the band used to tease me terribly about the tail but it was all good fun. Although I did once fall and break my arm and had to continue the tour with it in plaster.

It can't have been much fun for Tommy either as he was dressed in a leopard skin and carrying a club, which he had to wave around and threaten to hit me over the head with. Of course the girls all thought he looked great with his blonde quiff and flashing white teeth. He was a very good-looking boy and always had lots of female admirers. He said he thought I was 'a bit of a looker' and with his cockney charm insisted that the guys were all going mad for me.

The time I spent with the show was great fun and we all seemed to fit in well with each other I always had a laugh with Tommy. As did the rest of the cast, he was always good company and took everything in a very laid back way. I am pleased that Dave contacted me and asked me for a memory of that time. I look forward to reading the book I think it will be a good read about a really nice guy.

Lyn Cornell
Former Vernon Girl and Recording Artiste

Chapter Three

Tommy continued to make his boyhood journey through life and a wonderful bond was created with Rose and Connie that continues to this very day, in spite of events along the way that might have split apart less affectionate siblings.

A couple of years went by and it was time to move up to Royal College Street Secondary school. Of course that did not go smoothly for Tommy and his pals. As usual going along in a world of their own and not listening to a word anyone said. The five of them, who at that time were inseparable, Billy O'Keefe, Billy Gerrard, Ronnie Gibbs, Freddie Guntrip and Tommy just had a great summer holiday putting all thought of school behind them.

At the end of their holiday they all arrived at the Primary School, on the first day of the new term, only to be told by the headmaster that he despaired of them ever receiving an education, as they couldn't even listen to their teachers long enough to know that they had left primary school at the end of the previous term.

Of course the boys thought this was a great lark. Although the Headmaster and teachers at Royal College Street Secondary school were not impressed that the boys were late on their first day. This of course was no problem to Tommy and his pals, like most young lads school was not high on their list of exciting things to do. That phrase 'no problem' has gone on to be almost a catch phrase for Tommy, no matter what life throws at him he just shrugs his shoulders and says, 'ok, no problem', and gets on with things.

Times were very hard financially, in spite of Tommy's father doing two jobs and trying every way he knew to put food on the table. Although a basically happy family Tommy's parents were faced with a constant struggle to keep things on an even keel and understandably became tired as they tried to make ends meet. Because of that tiredness arguments would ensue and in the course of one of these arguments in her despair at the difficulties they faced on a daily basis Tommy's mum threw a knife in frustration. Although it had no intended direction, it caught Tommy's dad in the eye. He was taken to The Moorfield Eye Hospital in London but they were unable to do anything and so he was blind in that eye for the rest of his life. Tommy's mother was greatly upset by the damage her actions had caused and found it difficult to forgive herself. Tommy's dad on the other hand philosophically accepted his injury as just one of life's misfortunes and forgave her. He just continued with his life much as before and after a time within the family no reference was made about the eye. If as sometimes happened an outsider commented on it, Tommy's dad would just shrug his shoulders and say, 'oh I had an accident in the boxing ring when the rope caught me in the face and dragged through my eye as I fell causing cuts and abrasions to it'.

Tommy seems to have inherited his dad's philosophical outlook on life and to this day shrugs off misfortune, of which he has had more than his fair share, very often with the words 'oh well, that's life', or as previously stated: 'no problem'.

People were always on the lookout to make a few shillings by whatever means possible, Tommy's Uncle Bill, his mum's brother being no exception. He decided to take a few cases of tea from a local warehouse, involving Tommy's mum by using her back bedroom as a place to hide the cases. Although no-one realised it at the time, this decision would have tragic consequences.

As Tommy recalls Uncle Bill and his son, (who he thinks was also named Bill), carried the tea from the warehouse to his parent's house in Prebend Place and put it in the spare room. This part of the story became quite amusing; in fact in its day the story achieved legendary status around the local area.

It seems that one of the chests had a small hole in it, so causing the felons to leave a trail of tea right to the front door of Tommy's home. The police, without having to use much in the way of detection skills, had no trouble following it and they soon apprehended the gang.

At first having arrested Uncle Bill the police tried to involve Tommy's dad for receiving the stolen goods. He was totally unaware of what had gone on and protested his innocence and Tommy's mum was adamant that she, and she alone, was involved.

Things were to become a lot worse before they got better for the children. Found guilty and sentenced to a term in prison, Tommy's mum became ill and while in custody had to have a hysterectomy. Following the operation she had a coughing fit bursting all the stitches and started to haemorrhage. Despite the best efforts of those involved it was impossible to staunch the bleeding, to the point where losing blood faster than it could be replaced she slipped into a coma and died.

Tommy's dad received a telegram informing him of his wife's tragic death. Having previously absorbed everything that life had to throw at him, this news really was too much to bear as he had been hoping to bring her home soon. He was absolutely devastated, as was to be expected, so much so that he was never able to recover from the shock and his grief.

All Tommy remembers about this awful day is that his dad took him by the hand and set off for his nan's home. His dad cried all the way, unable to control his emotions, when they got there he collapsed saying, 'they've done her, they've really done her'. Being completely unable to cope with the loss of his wife, Tommy's dad was inconsolable and in this state he just gave up on life and pined away. To this day Tommy believes his dad died of a broken heart.

The bewildered children were struggling to cope with the death of their mother and, when their father's inability to come to terms with his terrible loss resulted in his own death, it seemed that life could not be worse. They were all passed to various relatives who in turn could not cope with the extra burden put upon them, and eventually the decision had to be taken, albeit reluctantly, to put the children into care. So the children found themselves in a Middlesex orphanage. The orphanage was called *The Ashford Residential School* and was situated in Woodthorpe Road, Ashford, Middlesex.

One of the things that was a real shock to Tommy as they got further out into Middlesex was this green stuff called grass and big things called trees. Tommy had never travelled far, only around the East End of London, and you don't find much in the way of countryside and greenery around there. In fact you could say that his popular recording of *Buttons and Bows* was styled to reflect how he felt about the countryside then and now.

Well chosen phrases such as *'don't bury me on this prairie, take me where the concrete grows'* and *'my shoes don't like the country hike cos the walkin' hurts my toes'* really just served to show how much Tommy has always loved his East End roots.

I know how much Tommy cares for Camden Town, as we still go down to Castle's pie and mash shop where he was first taken by his mum, as a very small boy, more than sixty-five years ago.

When we go it really is a homecoming for him people saying; 'Allo Tom alright, whatcha been doin?' and other similar greetings, reciprocated by Tommy. If people don't know him there they haven't been born yet.

Getting back to earlier times and the arrival of the children at the orphanage. Whilst obviously the reality of their arrival in the orphanage was a shock to all the children, Tommy found his first day there really traumatic to say the least.

Soon after his arrival the resident tough boy, one Peter Shilton, (not the future England goalkeeper), wanted to make Tommy aware of the pecking order there, so promptly set about him. One of the masters Mr Sims, separated them saying, "that's not the way we do things here." He then got the other boys to put some tables out to make a ring, put boxing gloves on them, and selected a second for them both.

Tommy's was a boy named Ali who advised him to go for the stomach, 'punch him good and hard' he said. So without delay they went at it. Southpaw Tommy ducking and diving saw his chance and released a tremendous blow to Peter's solar plexus knocking him to the ground.

Mr Sims picked Peter up and asked him if he wanted to continue, he said he did but as soon as they resumed Tommy repeated the blow and it was all over. Mr Sims asked Tommy who had trained him, as he had obviously had some coaching,

Tommy replied proudly, if a little sadly 'my dad'.

'Really,' said Mr Sims, mentally marking Tom down for the boxing team.

Tommy   Duffy Power

Billy Fury   Billy Fury
                               & Dickie Pride

Taken outside the gypsy's tent on Blackpool front

Tommy has been a good friend to me for many years and I take great pleasure in his company. He is a lovely man, with a warm sense of humour.

To me Tommy is the true professional, always turns up on time for rehearsals. There are never any big star tantrums and he always puts on a terrific show. I know how important it is to have the right person to manage you; I was fortunate to have Bunny Lewis by my side taking care of me from the very beginning. So I think Tommy has been very lucky to have Dave Lodge (the author) as friend and manager to guide him through his colourful career. Good, honest managers and agents are hard to come by these days!

Tommy is, as he has been all through the years that I have known him, A loveable cockney character who has not got an ounce of malice in him. Keep on rockin' Tommy you belong on the stage doing what you do best.

Craig Douglas.

Craig
Douglas

I first met Tommy in 1960 when he was touring with the Larry Parnes Extravaganza Shows. The show was on at The Empire Theatre in Liverpool and I went along because my brother (Billy Fury) was one of that stable of young pop stars and was also appearing. Also on the bill that night was Joe Brown, Dickie Pride, Johnny Gentle and top of the bill was Marty Wilde.

In those days, these types of shows would run every night for a week and I was fortunate to spend the whole week with them all backstage. In actual fact some of the boys used to stay at my parent's house in Liverpool so at times it was a "bit of a mad house" I can tell you. Pop stars everywhere you looked, so consequently I got to know them all pretty well.

Here is a short example of the kindness of Tommy back then. Tommy was going out with one of the Vernon Girls in fact most of the stars in that stable were going out with one or other of the Vernon Girls at one time or another. So, Tommy had gone off to Speke to take his girl home and it got kind of late so we all went to bed, locked up the house and assumed he would be back in the morning. Next morning I got up and got myself ready for work, there was still no sign of Tommy. As I left the house I saw Tommy's car in the driveway with him inside still fast asleep. He later told us that he was back late but did not like to wake us.

Life was so much fun and very exciting in those days, but as the years went by I lost touch with many of the stable stars (friends) and started to do my own shows as a tribute to Billy. This gave me an opportunity to work with some of those boys again and one of the first people I contacted was Tommy. Always reliable and a big, big hit with the audiences in fact I am also a big Tommy Bruce fan.

Tommy Bruce was, and still remains, a friend of the family. He is a true gentleman, a consummate professional and is still dazzling audiences to this day. Long may he continue.

Albie Wycherly

Chapter Four

The years passed by with Tommy getting into the usual scrapes for things such as scrumping apples and general mischief. A likeable boy he was well thought of by the other children as well as the masters who taught him. Surprisingly, particularly given his environment, Tommy succeeded in getting a sound academic education, due in part I think to him having an enquiring mind. Although never one to waste words he has grown into a very articulate man with a good understanding of the way the world works.

Although self-reliant to a high degree as a result of his time there, Tommy has a tendency to trust people who he thinks, very often mistakenly, know more than him. This has resulted in his being taken advantage of and also had his feelings hurt quite a lot during his life so far. That said it is also probably why he has such a lovely nature and attracts people to him with his quiet personality.

During his time in the orphanage he also excelled at sport; apart from the boxing he was an important member of the football and cricket teams. Any team event would find the other kids clamouring for Tommy's participation as his natural exuberance and enthusiasm was infectious and made for an enjoyable time.

Strange how in our young days sport was seen as a pleasant activity that could be character building and promote bonding and friendships that lasted long after our physical ability to take part in the games had passed. Whereas now it has often been viewed as being too competitive and promoting unpleasant and violent streaks in people. Even stranger then that we now live in the most violent period of our lives where some young people who had no access to competitive sport take delight in hurting the weak and elderly.

Anyway on with Tommy's story. Something that became a regular sight for the other masters during Tommy's time there was to see him standing in the corridor at least once a week. As they passed they would all smile and ask, 'music again Bruce?'

'Yes Sir,' Tom would cheerfully reply, because even at that young age his voice was so powerful it would disrupt any attempt the music master might make at communal singing. Little did any of them know that one day that powerful voice would bring him fame and fortune.

Tommy remained in the orphanage until 1952 when at the age of fifteen they placed him in a boys' hostel. When he left the orphanage the authorities, as was the normal way in those days, outfitted him with two of each item of clothing. This would include shirts, trousers, underwear, socks etc. They also found him a job in an engineering factory. Thus, as they thought, discharging their responsibility to each child in a caring way and giving them a start on the road to being a useful member of society

That was not quite how Tommy came to feel about things. He was nervous enough at being put out into the world to stand on his own two feet, his life so far had not prepared him for what was to come. When he started work Tommy thought he had landed in a Dickensian nightmare. He was absolutely terrified, as anybody would be by the horrors that faced him on the first morning.

The job he had been given was very unpleasant and frightening to say the least. Whether he liked it or not (and he didn't), he was forced to crawl underneath moving machinery in order to clean it. Of course he didn't dare refuse as his fear of the consequences, something that doesn't seem as prevalent in youngsters today, was even greater than his fear of injury.

To make matters worse at the end of each week most of his wages were taken from him by the hostel. Many children were hurt and maimed carrying out this dangerous job in factories up and down the country. In the light of the horror stories other workers there told him, maybe somewhat exaggerated, it did not take Tommy long to decide he ought to move on.

After making enquires and looking around he found himself a job on the delivery vans at *Smith's Crisps* and thanks to the husband of his mother's sister Ellen, his Uncle John who lived in London, he was also able to find accommodation, so leaving behind him the last physical attachments to the orphanage. Before long he was able to change jobs again with the help of the same uncle. Uncle John, John Ellis being his full name, worked in Covent Garden Market and he was able to arrange for Tommy to be employed there as well.

Tommy's birthday celebrations

Playing his latest song to Eddie Rogers

Tommy & Ken Platt

In late 1964 my group 'The Hideaways' were appearing at 'The Black Cat Club' in Carlisle when we had finished our spot, this gentleman who was 'topping the bill', said he was an R&B fan and had really enjoyed our set. He was a big name but not remotely 'big time'. His name was TOMMY BRUCE.

Fast forward some thirty years, after lots of water had flowed under many bridges and I find myself as compere of Rock 'n' Roll shows introducing regularly the indestructible Tommy!

It is immensely flattering to be asked to pen these few words to a truly wonderful entertainer who also happens to be one hell of a nice guy. (Not always the case in this BUSINESS of SHOW!) My grateful thanks to Dave Lodge, a man cut from the same cloth as Tommy, and somebody I regard as a good friend.

At the time of writing, the optimistic but cautious news about Tommy's health is good, and I hope, improving daily. I look forward to being able to introduce 'live' on stage as well as playing his records on my weekend Radio shows, the unique talent and personality of the original "London Boys"- Tommy Bruce.

Long may he keep on 'Misbehavin', on his own Rock 'n' Roll way!!

Frankie Connor
BBC Radio Merseyside

I remember Tommy Bruce from way back in the sixties when I appeared with him at The Northwich Memorial Hall. The Rolling Stones appeared that night although at that time they didn't top the bill; Tommy did. The Stones were very new to the business and I remember they were very smartly dressed, black trousers white shirts and black and white checked jackets. They didn't do very well as they were trying to educate the British audiences in the appreciation of very fine Blues music. That said they were brilliant the audience just wasn't ready for them.

Tommy came on stage and the crowd went wild for him and he did a great show. There was just one kid in the audience who had been heckling Tommy all night showing off for his mates about eight or ten of them. When Tommy came to do his last number the kid was still at it, Tommy just looked down at him and said 'just cos you're a right nana it doesn't mean you are one of the bunch!' The audience loved it and the lad's mates really gave him some stick.

I was standing in the wings and I thought this guy is a real professional a great act. I didn't see Tommy for many years and then one night at a gig in New Brighton this guy came up to me and said how much he had enjoyed my act and he thought I would work well in a show he was putting on for the guy he managed. The guy is Dave Lodge and the man he manages is Tommy Bruce. I appeared with Tommy in Leeds as Dave said I would and it was no surprise that Tommy Bruce is still a great act and more importantly to me he is a great guy. A real down to earth cockney my mate Tommy Bruce.

Lee Curtis

Decca Recording Artiste. Renowned for making more appearances at The Legendary Star Cub in Hamburg, than any other British act.

Chapter Five

It is more than likely that Tommy would have settled down in his job as a fruit porter in Covent Garden market and to his mind remained there for the rest of his working life. Indeed he has said that he would have probably continued in the market or got himself a little fruit and veg shop if he hadn't gone into show business.

However, National Service called Tommy in 1955 when he was eighteen years old, putting his life on hold for a couple of years. He joined The Royal Army Ordinance Corps and after his basic training he was stationed in Brookham camp near Antwerp in Belgium and worked in the stores. Apart from anything else, like all the other people conscripted at that time, he was taught how to drive, this skill would be very useful to Tommy in later times.

He soon became the smartest soldier on the camp as all the lads being demobbed would hand in their uniforms to him giving him the pick of the best kept ones, he would put his own items through the system so the British army was never short on the kit. I am sure that those readers who did national service remember how difficult it was to bring the rather basic and uncomfortable uniform and kit you were issued with up to the standard required by the Sergeant Major. Tommy cleverly spared himself a lot of hard work, also once again he showed how popular he could be in a group environment.

Leading an ordinary soldier's life he was prone to getting into a few scrapes most of his escapades involved returning late to camp after staying in *The Red Lion* pub for just one more pint.

The guards soon came to know and like the personable young cockney so much so that Tommy came to treat his stays in the guardhouse as a home from home, his mates used to provide him with cigarettes and bottles of beer to make his life more comfortable. They would pass him the items on the quiet, but Tommy says the guards knew but turned a blind eye.

Of course, as always with Tom, there was the odd problem with the ladies. Tommy did not see them as problems as they all loved him and he was more than happy to spend time in their company. No wonder in later times he would be nicknamed *Tommy Sweet Talk* by his friends. One of the problems he had with a young lady resulted in Tommy having to be transferred to the military prison at Baederfeld in order to avoid an irate father.

His problems all started when Tommy was reported absent without leave from the camp. Nothing could have been further from the truth. Tommy, having in his mind the idea of some privacy with his current young lady, decided a small island within the camp would be ideal. So with a few items such as blankets for their warmth and comfort he had set up his own camp in this small area, when this was discovered the charge was reduced to absent from his bed space.

Tommy was confident that this, in his eyes, relatively minor charge would have little effect on his army career, so he was in a cheery mood when he stood before his commanding officer. All a bit of a lark he thought. However his commanding officer soon corrected him on that score.

'This is a very serious matter Bruce,' he said. 'I have an irate father at the gate brandishing a shotgun and part of my brief is to preserve good relations with the local population. If I am not seen to take action in this case I could finish up with a riot on my hands. I must show that the British Army takes a dim view of this sort of thing, I have to be seen to take appropriate action. So Bruce do you accept my punishment?'

'Yes sir,' replied Tommy.

'In that case you will be shipped out to Baederfeld military prison for a period of three months.'

'But sir,' said Tommy, indignantly, 'I don't think that's fair, I never left the camp you know I didn't.'

'You agreed to accept my punishment didn't you?' His commanding officer asked ominously.

'Yes sir!' Replied Tommy.

'Right then, that's the end of it,' he said.

So Tommy left the camp under cover of darkness in a closed vehicle to start his sentence, once again his philosophical outlook stood him in good stead as he endured his incarceration. Mind you he was not so pleased when he discovered his three months would be added on to the end of his two-year service. Making sure that Queen and country got full use out of him.

In spite of this Tommy received a honourable discharge from the service. When his time was up he returned to England to await his discharge at the end of his national service. Of course even that could not be simple for Tommy. For several weeks he eagerly perused the bulletin board for his name, telling him he was going back to Civvy Street. After a while he got fed up and stopped looking, until one morning he was strolling through the camp when he heard a roar: 'That man, come to attention! What are you doing?' Asked the Sergeant Major.

'Going for breakfast sir,' Tommy replied.

'Breakfast!' said the Sergeant Major, 'you are not entitled to breakfast or anything else, and you shouldn't even be in the camp.'

Tommy had missed his demob date. How typical of the easy going young cockney that he should happily go about his daily duty when others were chomping at the bit so to speak, to get back into Civvy Street. This easy going manner has stood him in good stead right up to the present day, allowing him to accept, with a smile setbacks that would have broken many people.

When receiving his discharge, his commanding officer said of him; 'you have been a good soldier Bruce, in spite of your tendency to get into little scrapes, in fact I have no hesitation in saying you have been a credit to the regiment. I wish you well in future life.'

With his commanding officer's words still ringing in his ears when he got back to the UK, Tommy could not resist having one more bit of fun at the army's expense. Still in uniform, but not wearing his cap in the railway station, he was approached by two military policemen who instructed him to put it on; he refused, giving them the verbal runaround. He only told them he'd been demobbed at the point when they were about to arrest him.

Tommy did take a couple of mementos back to Civvy Street with him; his tattoos. 'What a loving keepsake from my army mates,' he says. 'They collared me one night after a few beers and dipping a darning needle in ink they wrote their names, it's a miracle that I didn't get blood poisoning. You can still see them, Doug, Tommy, Lloyd and Satch. My mates' names and my army number, 23278503, are all I have left to show for my national service with the R.A.O.C.' said Tommy, 'those two things and the never forgotten ability to bull my boots. People always ask 'where did you get the patent leather boots Tom?' The boys are all amazed that they are still the same leather boots that Annello and David made for me all those years ago. Lovely boots they make they look so good and they are so comfortable. All the boys Billy, Joe, Nelly and the rest, we all went there and had our boots made.'

In The Army Now!

Street Party at the end of World War Two
Tommy is the little boy on the left in top hat,
the costume he wore when he won the 5/- prize for singing
'Susie, sitting in the shoe shine shop'

Tommy Bruce is good company and someone who you look forward to being with; very few people have those qualities. Behind that gravel voice and his he man persona when you get to know him you will find a true cockney boy with venerability and a heart of gold.

I have lost count of the times I have spent working the provincial clubs and theatres that for all sorts of reasons, including the weather and the general feeling one gets when far away from home, times like that could have been unbearable. But with Tom around they will always be treasured memories never to be forgotten.

If someone wanted to know their way around the sixties music scene Tommy Bruce could give a master class. In an age when everybody wants to be a celebrity/star without making the effort or putting the work in, Tommy has been there done that and got the tee shirt and has the trophies, awards and gold discs to go with it.

There have been hit records, TV series, tours, concerts, summer seasons and now a biography written by his great friend and manager Dave Lodge. Yes Big Tom has, without doubt, made an enormous and lasting impression on show business and I am proud to have him as my pal.

Jess Conrad
Actor, Recording Star, Entertainer.

I have only known Dave Lodge for just over a year and I have found him to be a veritable mine of information when it comes to the music and the performers of the sixties. Give Dave the name of a top singer or group from that golden age and he will tell you that he has met them or worked with them! Ask Dave to arrange a radio interview with one of them and he will get back to you in ten minutes with it set up!

But Dave has other strengths as well, for a start he is honest and straightforward but, above all, he is loyal. To have a job that you love doing is a great asset and Dave Lodge clearly has great memories of his time on the road with Tommy Bruce and of the friendship that has grown between them over the years.

In the past year, thanks to Dave I have interviewed so many of the famous names from the sixties and each and everyone of them have recalled those happy days of the sixties and happy times in Dave's company. It is high time that Dave wrote a book about Tommy's life and his experiences and it is a right good read! If like me you reveled in the richness of talent available in the sixties, you will not fail to enjoy this record of what it was like to be part of those heady days.

Tommy Bruce was, and is one of my heroes. Tommy burst onto the music scene at a time and in a way that it would have been all too easy for him to have become besotted with it all but he didn't. To this day Tommy is modest about his achievements and is a really nice man to speak with. Above all he is a family man and proud to be so it is not surprising that he and Dave have never had a written contract in all the years they have been together.

Sometimes nice guys come second but I am pleased to say that Dave and Tommy can be proud of their achievements and their long lasting friendship. I wish Dave all the very best with this fascinating story.

John Pilgrim
Author and Broadcaster

Chapter Six

Tommy was soon back working in the market settling in and enjoying the life of a free and single young man. One of the first people he called to see was his Gran, she lived at 287 Royal College Street, Camden Town and when she saw him at the door she exclaimed "bleedin' 'ell look what the winds blown in, Winston Churchill will turn up next". Tommy knew he was home. He found himself a place to live in Notting Hill Gate, a basement flat, little knowing that his choice would change his life forever.

Returning to work in Covent Garden Market he soon fell back into the swing of things, out for a few beers with the boys at the weekend and chatting up the girls. Tommy had always had a fondness for budgerigars and dogs, so having his first real opportunity to have some to call his own, he chose to get these pets and move them into his flat. Tommy was happy in his life with no thoughts of changing things.

Even forty-six years later he still thinks fondly of them and remembers their names. There were the two Shelties, *Topsy and Brucie*, a poodle *Lindy Lou*, and *Bullie* a mongrel. On top of that he had two canaries, a parrot and, as he puts it, 'fifteen lovely budgerigars'. Tommy, when looking back says, 'it was a right bleedin' menagerie' but he actually said in print in 1960 that he would rather give up his contract than his pets.

He liked popular music; his personal favourites at this time were Johnny Ray and Anthony Newley. To this day Tommy can't believe that, with all the talent Anthony Newley had, he finished up with nothing, living in his mum's council house after being a millionaire at one time in his life.

Tommy Steele was another favourite, as he had shown it was possible to come up from a similar area to Tommy and be a great success. Tommy still has tremendous admiration for this versatile and hard-working performer. What a thrill it later gave him when Tommy Steele's own band *The Steel Men* backed him for his debut performance.

Sometimes Tommy would go along to the now legendary *21's* coffee bar and see the acts on show there. Terry Dene of course famously performed there, Cliff Richard and Wee Willie Harris were among the others who sang in the cafe. Little did Tommy dream that one day in the future sharing a stage with the likes of Terry, Cliff and Wee Willie would become the norm for him.

Tommy continued to go down there from time to time after he made his first record but the big difference between him and most of the other performers who went there was that they were hoping to be discovered so they could make it in show business, Tommy had already made it.

It was just great for Tommy having his own place with his own things around him, after being in the orphanage, the hostel and the army, for the first time since his parents died he had at last found somewhere that he could really say was his home. Being a likeable, friendly young man Tommy got on well with the other resident, who just happened to be his landlady, and when a new tenant moved in he would prove to be no exception to this.

A young man with ambitions to be a songwriter and a singer returned from America, determined to succeed in his chosen profession. The new tenant moved in upstairs initially with Pat, Tommy's landlady, Tommy was unaware that this man was in fact Pat's boyfriend. As time passed by, he and Tommy would become friendly. The young man was Barry Mason, and his opinion that Tommy had the looks to succeed in show business would change both their lives. In fact one day when Tommy was cleaning the car Barry asked Tommy if he would like to be a pop singer, typically Tommy just shrugged and replied, 'I don't know, I've never thought about it.'

As they got to know each other better, they went for a few beers, drank coffee together and generally socialised. Barry wanted Tommy to be more aware of what he was trying to do, so he invited him to come and see a recording session with a group he was managing and singing with down at the Mandrake Jazz

Club in Soho. Tommy thought it would be a bit of fun so went along with them. Of course in reality this was a bit of a ruse on Barry's part as he always intended Tommy to sing. At the end of the session there was still some time left so Barry asked Tommy if he would like to try his hand at singing.

At first Tommy refused but Barry kept at him. In the end he said he would give it a try although he only knew two songs, *'Why'* and *'Ain't Misbehavin'*. He didn't know what key he sang the songs in, but the piano player from the band, Tony Ross, of the *Tony Ross Trio* sorted that out for him, he enjoyed the experience, put it all down as a bit of fun went away and thought no more about it.

Tommy thought that Barry had taken the recording up to Norrie Paramour (recording manager for Colombia EMI), hoping he would be interested in the group, but as Barry has since told me the only interest he had in booking the recording session, was to get Tommy to sing. He just had a strong feeling that Tommy had what it took to get into the business even though he had shown no previous interest in singing.

When Norrie heard Tommy's voice he thought there was definitely something there, he identified Tommy's natural timing and rhythm. 'Is he a good-looking boy?' asked Norrie.

Barry, sensing that the door might just be opening replied, 'oh yes, this lad has got it all.'

'Right,' said Norrie, 'you had better bring him in to see me.'

Although he was very surprised when Barry asked him to go with him and see Norrie Paramour, Tommy went along feeling more than a little nervous. Norrie certainly liked the look of him and after talking to him for a short time asked him to sign a contract, which Tommy did.

Then Norrie said, 'what about a name?'

Tommy replied, 'what's wrong with Tommy Bruce?'

'Okay,' said Norrie, quite surprisingly really, with record companies at that time having a tendency towards names like *Fury, Wild* and *Power*.

Always easy going, as he still is to this day, Tommy's quiet manner made it appear that he was indifferent to the tremendous opportunity that had come his way. But inside he was in turmoil leaving the office in a bewildered state. 'Can this really be happening,' he asked of himself and Barry.

'Believe it Tom,' replied Barry, 'we are on our way.'

Even so the whole thing was just unbelievable, how could someone like him, with no thought of getting into the music business, have a recording contract? Why would anyone buy his records?

The questions kept flooding through his mind why should all these things be happening to him? It had all happened in a whirl, he kept thinking it must be a dream. 'I'll wake up in a minute,' he said to himself. He returned to his job in the market and for a while he really thought he must have imagined it, after all he reasoned nothing was happening. He could not have been more wrong.

After a few more listens to Tommy's voice, Norrie decided that '*Ain't Misbehavin'* was the song that they would go with for his debut disc. So he had Tommy come back in to re-record it with a rock cha cha arrangement. Then he decided that Ernie K Doe's number '*Got The Water Boilin*', would be on the flip side. I am sure that even in his wildest dreams Norrie could not have imagined the impact Tommy's voice would have on the record buying public.

Significantly for Tommy, Norrie's choice of '*Ain't Misbehavin'* had been in the charts for Johnny Ray at number sixteen in 1956. To record a song that had been sung by his favourite artiste made the whole experience even more special. When he actually climbed higher with his recording than Johnny Ray had done, he was both bewildered and ecstatic.

When the record was released Tommy had to appear on *Juke Box Jury,* the panel voted it a miss, in spite of their opinion it stormed into the charts. In those days some of the performers would be in a cubical off the set and much to the panel's surprise Tommy came out to greet them after their judgement, recovering from their shock they all wished him well in his career. A few weeks later it was Tommy's turn to be surprised, photographers and reporters descended on the market. He was still working there because as he says it was a good job, well paid and making the record had been fun but that was all. He couldn't possibly do that sort of thing for a living, could he?

The arrival of the photographers brought much delight to his fellow workers, who were teasing him with laughter and raucous cries of 'ain't she a luverly girl' to accompany every photograph taken. Tommy knew it was good-natured horseplay and accepted all of this in good part. In fact later when everything had calmed down, most of the guys said to him how proud they were that one of their number, was making a name for himself.

L to R: Don *the Gannet* McGinty, Pete *Mighty Mac* McGinty, Tommy, Peter Lee Sterling, Bobby Coral – The original Bruiser

I first met Tommy Bruce in terms of being in the business in Tin Pan Alley (Denmark Street) London when we were both there looking for songs. Although unlike any of the other boys I had been on nodding terms with him when he worked in the market.

I did a few shows with him in the early days and then we went our separate ways. I still bumped into him in the early seventies doing places like *Mr Smith's* in Manchester. He was always good company and I have never seen him give a bad performance.

When the sixties revival shows started I found myself on the same bill more and more often and would see him most weeks through the eighties into the nineties. Because of this we have become good friends. I like his cockney sense of humour and like me he enjoys the Teddy boys who still come along to see us to chat and dance, just like the old days.

I get on with his manager Dave as well, I like to wind him up by phoning him and pretending to be Tommy, we all have a good laugh about that. That's what the business is about having a laugh with your mates and Tommy is a good one.

Wee Willie Harris

I first met Tommy way back in 1960 when we were in a show together called *'We're No Squares'* at the Colston Hall, Bristol. The show was produced by my manager Robert Stigwood (his first production!!!) and Tommy was the star guest.

The show was compèred by Michael Medwin who was starring at the time in one of the most popular TV series of the day *'The Army Game'* I had just finished a TV series of my own for Granada called *'Biggles'* and Tommy was riding high in the charts with *'Ain't Misbehavin'*

I remember feeling very nervous as I was an actor and this was the first time I had sung on stage but Tommy gave me a lot of encouragement and a lot of laughs and it was with his help I got through the ordeal!

Tommy and I go back a long way. It's always a pleasure to see him and work with him and we still have a lot of laughs – He's a very special showbiz friend.

John Leyton

Chapter Seven

With the success of the record it was apparent that Tommy would have to go full time in the entertainment business and leave the market behind. With the help of his record company he would also be moving to a different flat, a very swish place provided by them. Petula Clark had been living there and Tommy was delighted to make her acquaintance before she left. He remembers her as being a very classy lady.

Of course to succeed in the business you need a quality agent and Tommy was no exception. It greatly helped his career at that time to be picked up by one of Britain's most prestigious agencies Fosters and to come under the auspices of Hyman Zahl. The work came flowing in once people got to hear of the down to earth and likeable young cockney.

One of the nicest things that happened to Tommy as a result of his success was a visit to his dressing room, after one of his shows, from one of the masters at the orphanage. He had brought a party of youngsters with him to see the show.

As Tommy shook hands with each of them in turn the master said, 'so you see boys, being in the orphanage is no restriction to success in life, if you apply yourselves anything is possible.'

Tommy was very proud to think that his former master saw him as an inspiration to the young people.

However Tommy's trip back to the orphanage some time later was not such a success. Arriving at the gate with a few gifts for the children he was stopped by a security guard. 'What's the problem asked Tom?' 'You can't come in here,' was the reply.

'Why not?' said Tom, 'I used to live here and just wanted to visit some of the masters and say hello to the kids.'

After more conversation it turned out that the orphanage had closed and the building was now a prison. The guard smiled and said, 'I don't mind letting you in but if I do I won't be able to let you out'. Having once been arrested on the old charge of loitering with intent, while waiting for a girl and not thinking too much of prison accommodation, he laughingly decided not to go in.

Tommy has always taken the view that it is no good having money if you don't use it to help the people you love. So one of the first things he did with his newfound wealth and fame was look after his sisters. He knew that Rose and Connie had taken Shirley in when she left the orphanage and they were all living back in Camden Town. Shirley, being younger, was the last one to leave the orphanage. Tommy did all he could to make sure each one of them benefited from his newfound success.

One of the sad things in Tommy's life was that Shirley was

destined to die young. She was struck down by cancer only about twenty years after she left the orphanage, in her mid thirties. In later years Tommy has questioned the hereditary nature of the disease given the impact it has had on both him and his sisters.

The next step in his career led him to set off with Barry at his side for his first live performance. The date was the 10th July 1960. It was on the *Mike and Bernie Winters Show* the venue was the Kemble Theatre, Hereford, he was backed by Tommy Steele's band *The Steel Men*.

This all came about following Tommy's appearance on '*Parade of the Pops*' with the great entertainer Tommy Steele himself. This was a great thrill for Tom who admired Tommy Steele so much. Also on the bill that night were Johnny Kidd and the Pirates. To say that Tommy was nervous would be an understatement - terrified would be a better word.

Johnny became a great friend of Tommy's, as did drummer Clem Cattinni, another of the guys who would remain a friend although not seen so often through the years was Brian Gregg. Like Clem he had been with Terry Dene in the beginning then working with other bands until they teamed up again in the Pirates.

As previously mentioned it was a nerve-racking and terrifying experience for Tommy. Bernie Winters kept introducing him, repeatedly saying, 'ladies and gentlemen Tommy Bruce,' but

Tommy was frozen in the wings. It seemed his career would end before it had even got started.

He was sick, he was cold, he just couldn't go on. Luckily Barry, who was just as nervous and had arranged for Tommy to go on with the microphone in his hand, said, 'look Tom it's alright just say Hello Doll like you do on the record and it will be fine.'

Funnily enough Tommy is still ice cold in the wings before every performance, even after more than forty-five years in the business he still reaches out to touch my hand, saying, 'feel how cold Davy'.

Also as Barry said to me when he came to see Tommy a couple of years ago, he himself experienced the same pain in the stomach he had experienced all those years ago at the Kemble Theatre, trying to get Tommy on stage.

Somehow Tommy managed to get out on the green and the place erupted, girls screaming, there was such a cacophony of noise Tommy couldn't hear himself. He was just part of the moment - he had arrived. The show was definitely on the road, to this day Tommy doesn't know if he sang or not. One thing was for sure; Tommy Bruce had arrived in show business, making an impact with his entrance that would set a standard for years to come.

My first job on leaving school in 1958 was with Keith Prowse records in Kensington High Street. When Tommy's record was released in 1960 it was so popular that we sold out our first batch in a morning.

I was amazed because having been brought up on Fats Waller I found it incredible that such a different arrangement of the song was proving so popular. Of course Norrie Paramour's Rock Cha Cha arrangement was very suitable for the beat generation that was coming through at the time. More importantly for me I liked it.

Exciting times and little did I know then that within five years I would move from the business of selling records to playing them and have my own part in the business.

Through my work as a DJ and in my capacity of show compere I met Tommy and found him to be a very nice chap. I look forward to reading the book his friend and manager Dave Lodge has written about him.

Ed Stewart

I have had the pleasure of knowing and working with Tommy Bruce for a great number of years and have always found him to be the absolute professional, both on and off stage. A great performer who always has time for his fans and a performer that is easy to get on with and a pleasure to work alongside. Attributes that, along with relentless hard work by his manager, Dave Lodge, have kept Tommy at the top of his profession for more than forty-five years.

They say that behind every good man there is an even better woman, Tommy's wife Ida is no exception. If this old adage is true then behind every successful performer is a truly great manager and Dave Lodge tops this category for me. Nothing is too much trouble for him, the service you get when dealing with him is second to none. Whilst looking after his artistes' needs he will always listen to promoters and help them to achieve their goals.

Dave's knowledge of the artistes of the period is phenomenal which I have witnessed when hearing him interview artistes, speak on radio and so forth. It should also be pointed out that that apart from being personal manager to Tommy, Dave is a much-underrated personality in his own right and a true gentleman in the entertainment world.

I most certainly am looking forward to reading Tommy's biography by Dave, knowing that it will be an in depth account of Tommy's life, career and the times and the people around him.

Alan Crowe AKA 'Ala Cra'
Sixties Revivalist, DJ, Writer and Promoter

Chapter Eight

Of course it wasn't long before Tommy had a thriving fan club, at first it was run by Barry's future wife, and Tommy's then landlady, Pat. As Tommy remembers it Pat ran his first fan club very well.

This was fine in the beginning but before long as the job became bigger he had two fan clubs, both of them were run by really nice young girls, one from Manchester, in the north of England, he recalls her name was Denise Palmer, the other was run by a southern girl called Vera Robinson who lived in Carshalton, Surrey. Tommy remembers them as being very enthusiastic girls with great personalities. He would love to hear from them again to find out what happened in their lives. I tried to contact them while writing this book but I was unsuccessful. If they buy the book and read this I would be happy to hear from them and put them back in contact with him.

One strange thing about Tommy's entry into show business came about as a result of Ronnie Varrel, a great drummer of the day, who actually performed up to his death, which only occurred a couple of years ago, in Frank Skinner's *Skinnerettes* band.

Ronnie, who was in the studio when that first acetate was made, (an acetate is a recording for demonstration purposes, which is only designed to last for about six plays), decided as a joke he would add the words 'and *The Bruisers*', after Tommy's name. He must have thought, like Barry, that Tommy looked like a middleweight and sounded a bit handy. Whatever the reason it was prophetic as it did indeed become the name of Tommy's band.

When Tommy was in Norrie's office that first day he was asked the question. '*The Bruisers,* that's your band is it?'

Somewhat confused Tommy just nodded and Norrie said, 'okay *Tommy Bruce and The Bruisers* it is.'

In actual fact it was not until Tommy did a gig in Birmingham at The Plaza Club some time later, and having been so pleased with the performance of the local band The Beachcombers, who had backed him so well, that he started to think that having his own band would be a good idea.

Tommy was very impressed by their performance so he asked if they would like to be his *Bruisers*, the boys jumped at the chance, another lucky thing was that their stage suits had a 'B' on the breast pocket. With the exception of Bobby Coral who we have all lost touch with, the boys are still Tommy's friends today. Mighty Mac in particular has been very helpful with my research for this book.

Tommy gave all the Bruisers nicknames. Peter Lee Sterling, on lead guitar who had a great voice, was affectionately known by Tommy as The Peanut, Pete (Mighty Mac) McGinty on bass named by Tommy for his muscular stature and prodigious strength. His brother Don (The Gannet) McGinty on drums, his insatiable appetite was legendary, and he never seemed to put any weight on, Bobby Coral (Tanner, as in the old sixpence), who would do some wonderful vocal harmonies.

Great days on the road with these guys, bass player Mighty Mac remembers the time after a gig at Diss in Norfolk when it could have all come to an end. Tommy and Barry Mason left first in Tommy's car, the boys set off a bit later with the gear.

Mighty Mac recalls it was dark and foggy driving on unlit winding, twisting roads. Suddenly, as they came round a bend they saw headlights from the hedge. Just managing to stop they saw Tommy and Barry staggering from the wreckage of the car, which had left the road as they came into an unseen bend. Miraculously neither of them were seriously hurt. Of course they all thought it was a great laugh, when you are young you never see the real danger in things.

One look at the car was enough to tell them it was going nowhere. Barry and Tommy got into the van and off they went again. Only stopping at the first phone box to call for a recovery vehicle, no mobile phones way back in the sixties, then it was home to London, the car was never seen again. To this day Tommy cannot remember if he or Barry was driving.

It seemed quite remarkable that Tommy could see a car go without missing it when only a short time before, while still working in the market, he was pleased to own a car, never mind not be worried if he wrecked one. How times had changed for this happy-go-lucky lad. He was having a great time and every day just seemed to bring more fun. Compared to being in the market and getting up at the crack of dawn, travelling about to do this singing lark, although tiring, couldn't be work could it?

Another laugh the boys had was at Scunthorpe Baths Hall in the early sixties. They played there on a few occasions. There was a low beam at the back of the stage, which did not allow the drummer to sit up straight and Don the Gannet hit his head several times. Of course Tommy, ever the comedian, said, 'look Gannet I know you're hungry, but you don't have to try and eat the bleedin' theatre.'

A guitarist called Craig Austin who was often in the audience for shows at this venue, (He now plays in a duo called the Beverley Brothers) told me it was worse when the Honeycombes played there. He said that once Honey Langtree hit her head so hard she couldn't continue playing. Having met with, and also compèred a show, with that lovely lady performing on it, I can only say it must have been a hard hit, because she is a real trouper, who always copes with any adversity.

Another venue Tommy remembers with great affection is The California Ballroom in Dunstable. He and the Bruisers enjoyed appearing there, he says it was a legendary venue where all the great names have appeared over the years and you were always sure of having a good time.

Fender the well known guitar makers supplied the Bruisers with instruments and amps. This made them a very impressive looking and sounding outfit, as they were all exceptional musicians. Pete still has, and performs with, his guitar today.

The boys went on to have their own top twenty hit '*Blue Girl*'. As a songwriter Peter Lee Sterling wrote some wonderful songs including '*I Think Of You*' and '*Don't Turn Around*' for the Merseybeats and Kathy Kirby's second placed song in the Eurovision song contest '*I Belong*'. He also had a successful solo career as Daniel Boone.

Bobby Coral sang with The Ivy League, after the Bruisers had split up, using, we believe, the name John Ship. Pete McGinty and his brother Don played with some local bands in the London area and, as they put it, concentrated on the day job. It should be noted that the Bruisers led the way for other successful bands that came out of Birmingham.

Also Peter Lee Sterling was a great influence on the type of songs being performed in the sixties and seventies. He is another of those artistes who would only have a relatively small amount of success, when looked at in relation to the amount of talent they possessed.

Tommy Bruce & The Bruisers

Nelly, George, Tommy and fans

TOMMY
BRUCE
AND
THE
BRUISERS

Adoring fans

Jimmy Phillips introduces Lilli

Eddie Rogers, Jimmy Phillips
head of KPM

Tommy and Peter Lee Sterling

At the piano

Tommy, Hank Locklin and Frankie Vaughan

Absolutely Unique! That is the way I have always thought of Mr Gravel Voice - Tommy Bruce.

I have had the pleasure of working with Tommy over many decades including once when I was doubling in a nightclub. Tommy is a real showman and always has us rolling around with laughter, with his infectious sense of humour.

Ain't Misbehavin' began my love of his fabulous voice, and I always sat down to watch '*Stars and Garters*' to see Tommy (and Kathy Kirby as well!!!) recordings like '*Horror Movies*' and '*Monster Gonzales*' suited Tommy's style so well and really should have been big hits in their day also really enjoyed the B-sides '*I'm on Fire*' '*The London Boys*' and '*Got the Water Boilin'*'.

Live shows with Tommy have always been great fun to be part of. From his off stage shout of 'Hello Baby' (his intro to *Chantilly Lace*) through to his hits of '*Ain't Misbehavin'*' '*Lavender Blue*' and his one EP version of '*Shakin All Over*' and all the other numbers that when performed by Tommy, have become his own.

Over the years it has never ceased to amaze me just how powerful his voice is. The unique volume and tone have never diminished, his banter with the audience and some wonderful off the mike comments to his musicians are always amusing I know that my fellow Rapiers and myself always look forward to working with Tommy for the great times we have and the fact that Tommy is such a genuine down to earth artiste.

It is a delight that Tommy has continued with his stage show over all these years and a privilege to have worked alongside a true sixties original.

God bless you Tommy - A great artiste and a perfect gentleman.

I must say a big thank you to Dave Lodge for his support of Tommy over the years and for writing and getting this book published. It will be welcomed by Tommy's fans, which definitely includes me and my wife Janet (who adores him!!)

Colin Pryce-Jones, The Rapiers

Most hit parade performers of the late 1950's early 1960's, presented themselves in the Elvis mould of endeavouring to be sensual and moody. Artistes appearing on the concert tours would fight to be the first to rehearse and stake their claim to sing one of the American classics such as, *Jailhouse Rock, Whole Lotta Shaking, Be Bop A Lu La* and *It's Only Make Believe* to name but a few.

The Brylcreamed quiff, the gold lamé jacket, the black shirt and white shoes were all a familiar part of the turnout for most who wanted to be, or thought they were, heirs to the Elvis throne.

It was a like a breath of fresh air when, during the rehearsal for a Sunday concert, a young, happy, personable, un-Elvis-like character, walked onto the stage and began singing the evergreen, *"Ain't Misbehavin"*.

The voice was so different and distinctive you couldn't help but take notice. This was something new! No problems with this guy's repertoire. No concerns of him having to get in first to sing the American classics his peers would be fighting to make theirs for the night. There was a new and refreshing kid on the block. This guy was not only different, he was good!

From the first time of meeting Tommy Bruce you couldn't help but want to be his mate. His relaxed manner, his charm, his most unusual vocal style and his wonderful sense of humour put him apart from the rest.

Tommy didn't want to be an entertainer. He already was! He wasn't a threat. He was an asset! His performances were always the pinnacle of professionalism and his work ethic left nothing to be desired.

For over 45 years Tommy has come across to his audiences like an old friend. To his fellow performers he is, and always will be "Tom Tom", the gravely voiced pal with the heart of gold.

When you have read this book I'm sure you will feel as if you've known "Tom Tom' as long as the rest of us lucky ones have.

Vince Eager

Sixties Television and Recording Star, International Entertainer.

Colin Pryce Jones

Vince Eager

Chapter Nine

No sooner had Tommy made his first appearance, to such resounding success and public acclaim, than he found himself in Blackpool for the summer season. Larry Parnes had seen and heard about this new sensation with his gravel voice and thought Tommy was just what he was looking for for his new show.

Larry's confidence in Tommy was so high that when the great Gene Vincent was unable to appear due to his daughter, Melody, sadly dying, Larry had no hesitation in putting Tommy in Gene's place.

This had been a terrible time for Gene, as he had also had to suffer the loss of his friend and fellow performer Eddie Cochrane in a car crash. Gene himself had been injured in the same crash and was not fully recovered. Indeed in the week previous to his daughter's death he collapsed before his Saturday night performance at the Glasgow Empire and had to be taken to hospital. Although he returned for future performances he was far from fit.

Larry Parnes was in no doubt that Tommy was the man for the job and so had no hesitation in putting him on the bill. It was never even considered that they needed to put a more experienced artiste in Gene's place as Larry regarded Tommy as one of the most natural entertainers around.

Of course Tommy looks back now and thinks, as he did then, about the tragedy that seemed to run through Gene's life, but as he says these were exciting times for him and he just felt honoured to be considered worthy to replace an artiste of Gene's talent. Tommy would have wished for happier times for Gene, but had to take the opportunities that came his way. As Gene himself said to Tommy later, 'no worries Tom somebody had to get the gig I'm glad it was you'.

The show was *'Idols on Parade'*; the venue for this significant step up in Tommy's career was the Queen's Theatre, Blackpool The date 17th July 1960. Rarely can there have been an artiste who was catapulted to the top of the entertainment ladder with such speed and more importantly so little preparation.

Tommy appeared in this show with Joe Brown and Peter Wynne, who, Tommy still believes should have been a massive star, as he says Peter's voice had an operatic quality. Tommy would listen to him in the dressing room going through his scales and wonder how can it be that this boy is not having hit after hit.

More than once Tommy remembers Peter stopping the show with his wonderful voice. Also appearing was Nelson Keene who was to become Tommy's great friend. The first time Nelly saw

Tommy was at the rehearsal, Tommy sang *'Great Balls of Fire'* with all the other acts sitting in the front row and they all gave him a standing ovation.

The same thing happened when Nelly sang, after this he and Tommy just hit it off and as they shared dressing rooms they would always go to the wings with each other. Tommy would always say 'Kill em Nelly' as he went out on stage with Nelly offering the same encouragement to Tom when it was his turn. In fact although they have been seperated by thousands of miles for over twenty-five years since Nelly emigrated to Australia, I found when I traced him that the affection created by that friendship was not diminished by time or distance. I am pleased to say that they are back in touch and neither Nelly nor Tommy want that contact to ever be broken again. My conversations with Nelly have shown me exactly why Tommy made him his friend he is a great guy.

We must not forget Lance Fortune and Georgie Fame two guys who were making their own mark in show business. Lance went on to have success I believe with the comedy vocal group The Ugly's, but he has had serious health problems in recent years, having had several strokes. This has deprived us of the chance to see him on any of the numerous package shows, which have toured the country over the last few years. We wish him good health in the future. Georgie Fame has enjoyed great success over the years both as a successful chart artiste and as a live performer.

Backing for the guys was provided by Nero and His Gladiators, a band who were, at that time, achieving their own deserved popularity with the fans, the show was compèred by the very talented vocal impressionist Billy Raymond.

They performed in matinee shows throughout the summer. Part of the show required the cast to dress up as girl guides, Joe Brown acting as troop leader. The sight of Tommy in short skirt, jackboots and a long black wig takes some imaging.

On one occasion Larry Parnes was there with a cinè camera filming the show. The Girl Guide sketch required the 'girls' to number off under instruction from Joe. One, two, three, four, all replied in suitably camp voices, Tommy looking like a demented apache with head band and motorcycle boots to set off the obligatory short skirt, then bellowed five in his gravely voice. The audience were in fits, and his fellow performers collapsing with laughter. Great stuff!

Larry however, to quote Queen Victoria was not amused, so he cut Tommy's performance from the film. He was extremely annoyed and quite adamant that Tommy had to toe the line in future. He had no chance; Tommy's natural exuberance is what makes him the great performer that he is, so he continued to wow the audiences with his unorthodox approach to everything. He continues to stamp his own style and authority on every performance to this very day.

In the evening the legendary George Formby appeared at the theatre, George and Tommy got on well and George wanted to give Tommy a beautiful ukulele. It was inlaid with mother of pearl, Tommy remembers George and the ukulele well, but being a shy unassuming lad, he was too embarrassed to take it, something he has always regretted as it would have been a wonderful memory of the great man.

One of Tommy's other memories of George was of all the fans that waited outside to see him. He used to have great trouble getting through them after his show, so on one occasion Tommy said, 'don't worry George, I'll be your muscle and get them to make way for you.' From George's point of view, the powerful young cockney was very successful holding the fans back to good effect. However, as Tommy says, for him it was a mistake as he emerged from the melee with his shirt torn, his hair almost pulled out by the roots and scratches all over his face and neck, as the girls tried to get souvenirs of him. He has often remarked on this to others like Billy, Nelly and Dickie and he wonders why, if the girls liked them so much, did they want to cause such pain?

Tommy became so popular in this holiday resort, that the great northern impresario Douggie Chapman would make regular demands on Tommy's services. I recently went up to see Susan Maughan in one of Douggie's promotions. In the course of conversation while having a drink after the show, Douggie gave me the impression that he still has fond memories of Tommy as a performer. John Leyton would also appear in Blackpool with Tommy as part of another package show.

There was another occasion that springs readily to Tommy's mind, when he was called upon to replace Gene Vincent. This was on the now famous first 'Rock Across the Channel Show', where the acts performed all the way across the channel to France. It is memorable for the fact that Tommy appeared on *Brian Matthew's Saturday Club* in the morning and then made a frantic dash to catch the ferry and be part of the onboard show.

One of the main acts on that trip was *The Shadows*, a band for whom Tommy still has great admiration. In fact he still considers Jet Harris to be a close friend. He admires Jet for the way he has overcome the difficulties he has met in life and for having success not only with *The Shadows* but also in a duo with drummer Tony Meon who sadly died in a fall in his home whilst I was writing this book. We also see Bruce Welch quite often on our travels and Tommy both likes and admires him.

Some of you may have read elsewhere that a different artiste was on this trip but I can assure you that it is a matter of record that Tommy did replace Gene and he did perform in the show and for him it was a wonderful experience. These were very exciting times for Tommy and he could not believe the welcome he was getting whenever and wherever he appeared.

One of the coincidences in the music industry comes along here in connection with Tommy knowing Tony Meon because, Tommy's son who is a very talented singer song-writer who as yet has not received the acclaim his talents deserve, was part of a band with Tony Meon's son having met each other quite by chance and recognised each other's ability. Unfortunately due to the vagaries of the music industry their band was not successful and split up.

Christmas card signed
by Larry Parnes

I first met Tommy in 1984 at a charity gig in north London. I was embarking on a solo career after my band 'Matchbox' had decided to break up. I was the last of the original five members we had achieved chart success having had seven hit records from 1979 to 1983. My good friend Dave, the late Screamin' Lord Sutch had encouraged me to go solo and got me on many Rock 'n' Roll package shows. I was introduced to Tommy by Gene Vincent's ex wife Margaret.

When Tommy and I spoke we talked about what I had done, me seeing him on television when I was younger and also the fact that my brother Ken Rankin had backed him on bass once. On all the shows at the various venues it was always Tommy's good humour that kept the cast laughing and he would help anyone out when needed. On these bills I met The Vernon Girls, Terry Dene, Jet Harris, Wee Willie Harris, Don Lang, Mike Berry, John Leyton and many others. My impression of Tommy was that he was a nice person who was always friendly and helpful to others.

We worked on a lot of the Butlins 50's and 60's weekends in Bognor Regis and Pwllheli, North Wales and several others. When he met my future wife Caroline he joked with us that as he was in the next chalet we kept him awake all night at Bognor.

In 1987 Tommy got Caroline and I a two-week working holiday in Calpe Spain. An English guy Rory Wild and his wife who live in Spain ran the shows and we were there with Terry Dene and his wife Linda. Tommy and I stayed friendly after that although we did not work together very often on shows. He always remained warm and friendly when we did meet up.

Although 'Matchbox' have now reformed I still keep my solo options going and in 2004 Tommy was on the same bill as 'Matchbox' for two shows. One was the Eddie Cochrane Weekender at Chippenham and the other was at a holiday camp in Rhyl North Wales. I was very happy when Tommy and his manager and friend Dave Lodge stayed to watch me perform with Matchbox.

Tommy is one of the nice guys in show business and I am glad to know him as a friend. I am grateful for the opportunity to write this for the book and I wish Dave and Tommy every success with it. I am sure that it will be an interesting look at the early days of our music and of our Tommy Bruce. God bless, regards and best wishes always dear friend.

My thanks go to my daughter Chrystal for her assistance in helping with the text for this book, also to my son Vincent for keeping us amused with his attempts to help too. My wife Caroline sends her good wishes To Tommy and my thanks go to her for always being there to help with everything.

Graham Fenton

Chapter Ten

Returning to the story the speed of Tommy's success was incredible, his powerful voice, cheerful demeanour and let's not forget his dashing good looks were sending audiences wild. The strange thing was, unlike some of the other performers at the time Tommy's appeal was, as it is today, universal.

The girls were crazy about him, the Teds liked him because of his down-to-earth good humour, and stranger still, parents liked him. My mum thought Tommy was great yet she wasn't keen on Cliff Richard and that was a typical response that Tommy got all across the country.

As a live performer Tommy is second to none. With different management ideas both at the height of his success and later in his career, there is no doubt in my mind and that of many others that with his talent he would have developed into one of this county's greatest all round entertainers. His versatility and warm personality should, with the right career choices have ensured his success in musical theatre and encompassed a much wider television career.

Of course pantomime beckoned for Tommy and he always enjoyed the actual shows, as he was able to give free rein to his exuberant personality. He loves anything that requires audience participation and even in his own cabaret and rock and roll shows always involves the audience to a high degree. But he always found it particularly arduous rehearsing for pantomime, particularly on some occasions where he felt that the pleasure was being taken out of a particular scene. So much so that on one occasion he called the agent who got him the gig to say he wasn't happy.

'Never mind Tom,' said the agent, 'just put it down to experience.'

Tommy growled in his gravely voice 'it's an experience I could bloody well do wiv out.'

As a result of clashes like this Tommy choose not to appear in pantomime for many years.

One of the things that has really annoyed him over the years is people's efforts to compare him to other artistes. At various times they have tried to label him, because of the songs that Norrie chose for him to record, as the new Fats Domino, Fats Waller and of course The Big Bopper.

As Tommy has said, he had heard of them, but was not aware of their recording or the arrangements of them, at the time he made his. In fact some of the people who have tried to make these comparisons were not even born at the time of Tommy's recording career. In the beginning Norrie, and then Charles Blackwell, would do the arrangements for the song with Tommy having no say about it, so how could he, a boy from the market as he put it, have any idea what the finished product would sound like. One thing is certain, people can suggest as often as they like that Tommy copied one artiste or another and there is very little that we can do about it, but perhaps they can explain why in spite of many people contacting me for help in preparing to go on *Stars in Their Eyes*, no one has yet succeeded in sounding like him. The truth is he is simply unique and some people struggle with that idea as their view of life requires labels to be stuck on everything and everybody. They are frightened by what is different and so try to rationalise and compartmentalise people and things so that they look intelligent and in control. Tough luck to all of them Tommy Bruce is still defying their kind of description forty-six years down the line.

For example it was because of Johnny Ray that he knew *'Ain't Misbehavin'*, for no other reason except it was the only version he knew and he liked it. Norrie said they were going to re-record it with a rock cha cha arrangement, Tommy freely admits he didn't even know, at that time, what a rock cha cha arrangement was.

Tommy eventually stopped contradicting DJs and others who claimed to know better than him why he had recorded certain songs. On one recent CD the guy who wrote the sleeve note commented that Tommy was a cross between Howlin' Wolf and Doctor John. Tommy was incensed, as he said to me, 'quite apart from the fact that the guy has taken the résumé that you wrote about me more than twenty years ago Davy and copied it, I just don't know who these two geezers are that he mentions. I think I might have heard of Howlin' Wolf but I don't know any of his songs and as for Doctor John, I really don't know, is he one of the new boys? What's the matter with these people why can't they just say I'm Tommy Bruce?'

'Never mind Tom,' I replied, 'it just goes to show that as hard as they have all tried, they just can't categorise you and that means you will never be forgotten.'

That distinctive gravel voice is incomparable and he has the most wonderful stage presence. Some of the young performers today could do a lot worse than have a look at Tommy's live show, if they did they would learn a lot.

It has to be said that some strange things happened with Tommy's recording career. His contract with Columbia stated that he was signed to them in perpetuity, yet he recorded for other labels in the sixties. Also a question I have repeatedly asked of EMI is, if the contract is in perpetuity then when are they recording his next album? I have yet to receive a satisfactory answer. All I do know is so far; no lawyer has been able to find a way of breaking the contract.

Polydor recorded '*Boom Boom*' and '*Can Your Monkey Do The Dog*'. He was the first British artiste to record for them but they had no distribution network in the UK so the recording was almost unheard at the time.

I approached Polydor a couple of years back to ask them if they wanted to repay Tommy for his faith in them all those years ago by putting out the recording now as *'Boom Boom'* always stops the show when he performs it in his live act these days. As is usually the way in this business my request was met with complete disinterest.

CBS went one better and recorded four songs, *'I guess I've Been Around Too Long'*, *'The Colour Of The Soil Is Different'*, *'The Reason Why'* and *'Heartbreak Melody'*. The record company released two but strangely put no promotion behind them so there was no opportunity to see if they would be hits. Then the other two remained in the vaults unheard for nearly forty years, until they were re-recorded for a CD that was put out in 2000.

Given Tommy's poor memory with regard to some of his recordings from all those years ago it may be that some of these companies have more recordings in their vaults that we don't know about and that nobody will ever hear.

I should mention that a wonderful man called Max Diamond wrote the songs, beautiful ballads were obviously his speciality. They all certainly suited Tommy's voice and should definitely have been heard by a wider audience.

Max had a varied career in show business. Prior to his death about eight years ago I believe he acted out the role of a Knight in jousting contests, at theme parks like Camelot, indeed some people credit him with having been one of the innovators of this kind of entertainment. Tommy remembers him with great affection.

The fans who bought the CD said that anyone of these songs could, indeed should, have been as big a hit as '*Ain't Misbehavin'* in the sixties. Of course there are many other artistes with a similar story to tell of chances missed by recording companies.

Perhaps the strangest recording of all was made for RCA Victor '*Monster Gonzales*'. This was made as a spoof of the American singer Pat Boone's hit '*Speedy Gonzales*' Specifically for the American market, but once again wasn't released.

Strange, the reason given was that his cockney accent wouldn't sell there. Funny, he had the accent when they asked him to record it. Funnier still, his CDs sell in America now, I know this because I receive emails from the people who buy them. Once again it is a story of chances not taken and opportunities missed. Tommy said, 'I don't know why they didn't release it, but it certainly had nothing to with my accent as people still like it after all these years.'

Two of his recordings stunned the music press just when they thought they had him catagorised. The first one to take everybody by storm was '*Babette*'. Charles Blackwell, the man who had been creating the arrangements for John Leyton stepped up for this one. Indeed a quote from the music press of the day said, *'this is the record that finally establishes the Tall Silent Boy, Charles Blackwell as the Musical Director of the day'.*

The young guns of the music world today who think they are doing well should realise that in the opinion of many, Charles Blackwell was the best of them all, having achieved this outstanding success by the time he was just twenty years of age. There is no doubt that with this record any thoughts that Tommy Bruce was a gimmicky singer were dispelled. The backing had an unbelievable orchestration unsurpassed in the UK and America.

Reviews included *'Babette Is A Thumping Big Hit'*, *'It's called Babette And It's Great! Great! Great!'* *'This Is A Thumping Big Hit!'* Headlines like: *Read All About It. That Tommy Bruce Boy Can Really Sing* sprang from newspapers everywhere. DJs and music journalists alike were just blown away by the recording.

Ronnie Varrel a great drummer whose career spanned over fifty years was betting everybody who would take him on £25 that it would be an unforgetable recording and a massive hit. It has certainly stood the test of time and is still recognised as one of Tommy's finest recordings.

Another innovative recording was *'Over Suzanne'*. This song with Big Jim Sullivan on lead guitar was the first to feature a fuzz box, this piece of equipment is best remembered for recently being used by Cher on her hit recording *'Believe'*. Once again Tommy gave an outstanding vocal performance that received rave reviews. He is only now being fully recognised for the quality of some of his finest recordings.

Of course to this day we suffer from the intransigence of the recording companies. The young executives today seem to find it impossible to believe there is a record buying public out there over the age of sixteen. Completely overlooking the large fan base that keep attending the shows of people like John Leyton, Craig Douglas, Marty Wilde, Joe Brown and Tommy, and who would love, as they keep telling us, the chance to buy and listen to the music of their favourites.

These same young executives who will happily make money out of someone else's efforts to put the artistes out on CD on the basis that you must buy a licence off them because the artistes contract was signed in perpetuity. Completely failing to see that the contract and the words therein constitute a two-way street and they should morally, if not legally, still be looking after their artistes needs.

However, on with the story we must not allow children who were not even born when the artistes from the fifties and sixties laid the foundation for their work opportunities today, to detract from the story of what Tommy has achieved.

The new brusiers: Steve Bryd, Mac Poole, Tommy,
Roger McKue and Pete Windle

Chris Black, Peter Stockton, two un-named fans, Tommy, Heinz and Don Lang

Tommy and I met each other on Jack Good's "Wham Show" where people voted for their favorite stars by post. Now they do it by phone nothing much has changed. I have great memories of Tommy on stage dressed in loud colours and lots of jewelry. A true showman.

In the early sixties Tommy had his first hit and it was a big one, massive in fact with *'Ain't Misbehavin'*. I started in show business and we went on a theatre tour together.

I was bottom of the bill (the poster printers' name was in bigger letters than mine). Tommy was top of the bill and had the number one dressing room at his disposal, I didn't have a dressing room so Tommy agreed to share his with me. I took this gesture as a great honour. To me this showed his generous nature and is just one reason why Tommy is still a much loved artiste in the biz, not just by the public who adore him but especially by his fellow pros.

Thank you Tommy for your encouragement and your friendship. You are the old school and a true gentleman.

Danny Rivers
Top Rank recording artiste.

It is a strange thing in this show business world that some of us inhabit, from the outside it always looks glamorous. People think how great it must be when we all get together for a big special show, a charity, or a royal occasion – well it is. But the truth of it is that unless it is for something special, singers don't often work together. In fact it can be a very lonely existence on the road, performers are like ships that pass in the night as it were.

Of course we do meet from time to time socially but I feel, not as often as people might think. Another situation that can bring a bunch of singers together is TV. It was only through a very successful television show called *Stars and Garters* that I met Tommy Bruce and got to know him. Up to that point I only knew of him through hearing his records and from the odd guest appearance on a radio show we used to do called *Parade of the Pops*.

I am sure Tommy won't mind me saying this but I feel that he should have sustained his popularity more than he has. It seems to me that our business is now too full of celebrities who are famous for being famous but have no talent. Leaving people like Tommy with real talent to be constantly overlooked. In some ways I think Tommy suffered like me from having a really big hit, in his case *Ain't Misbehavin'*, in mine *Edelweiss*. What happens is that people perhaps have a job to get past that and it becomes difficult to move a career along. Another important thing, maybe the most important in an artiste's career is being with the right management. Happily I think this has come to pass for Tommy since he has been with Dave Lodge. I know that Tommy has not been in the best of health for some time but he seems to have come through that now and he is recuperating as I write this.

So here's to many more years Tom - keep hanging in there - our business needs you.

All my best wishes.

Vince Hill

Chapter Eleven

People in show business were sitting up and taking notice of the likeable and talented young cockney, Radio and television appearances were becoming the norm. Under the auspices of the great innovator Jack Good, Tommy was soon part of the great teen shows of the day. *'Thank Your Lucky Stars'* was a tremendous show compared by Brian Matthew. Tommy remembers one of the line-ups for this show and it is sensational. Apart from Tommy himself, the line up included John Leyton, The Bachelors, Peter Noble, Jackie Trent, Julie Grant, Kenny Ball and Bobby Curtola. The great thing about this show is that there was a line up like this every week with a host of different names.

ATV had a great Saturday night show called *'Tin Pan Alley'*. Once again featuring different artistes every week showing the depth of talent in the UK in the sixties. Tommy appeared with Jackie Chan, Roy Castle, Frankie Vaughan and Johnny Worth and they showed excerpts from the film musical *L'il Abner* to complete the show that night bandleader Jack Parnell was the musical director. As a spin off from that Tommy did a twenty minute interview for a programme called 'Face In Focus' talking about his rapid rise to fame in show business.

As always being very modest about his own talents Tommy marvelled at the talent of his co-stars. For example among the musical talents at the time Johnny Worth had written songs for Adam Faith, Tommy had the pleasure of working with Adam and he liked him very much. It was really sad news for Tom when he heard that Adam had died.

Tommy recalls always being in awe of Roy Castle's ability to play such a variety of musical instruments and he also said what a lovely man. Charming and courteous and not the slightest hint of the arrogance that other people with less talent might show.

Frankie Vaughan just looked as though he was born to be a star, very handsome with a great voice and displaying great charisma. Also says Tommy, Frankie was a charming and very friendly man and he enjoyed his company on the many occasions they were together. Whilst we were talking about Frankie, Tommy was reminded of another charismatic star with a powerful voice, someone who he liked and admired very much: Dickie Valentine. Dickie was another of Tommy's friends in the business who sadly died in a car crash and is still missed by friends like Tommy and fans everywhere.

It may have been for his sense of humour, as well as his singing ability, that Tommy was cast in the ATV show 'I Feel Fine.' I place this show here to show the longevity of Tommy's television career. Hosted by Stan Boardman, it combined humour and music in a way not seen on television today. Other stars appearing were Gerry and The Pacemakers, The Vernon Girls, making a one off appearance, Dave Berry, Richard Stilgoe and Mick Miller.

This show went out more than twenty-five years after Tommy recorded *'Ain't Misbehavin'* showing that the novelty singer was no such thing as he was still in great demand. As he would be today if television still showed the proper variety shows that people of my age crave. The BBC or any other station would do well to employ the talents of Ernest Maxim to teach the young producers of today what works in television entertainment before it's too late.

'Wham' of course was another great show, not to mention 'Top of the Pops', 'Now Dig This', 'Six Five Special', 'Oh Boy', and 'Drumbeat' which really brought the tall good-looking Vince Eager to the public's attention, and 'Saturday Club' where Tommy almost became resident, he appeared so many times. All these shows giving Britain's youth the chance to thrill to the performances of Tommy and his contemporaries. While he was appearing on the 'Wham' show Tommy met Sheila Prytherch the lovely Liverpool lass, who would one day become his wife.

Up to this point Tommy had been meeting and romancing some very attractive girls and getting to know them. Girls from in and out of show business. Girls like Alma Cogan, *the girl with the giggle in her voice* and the previously mentioned Petula Clark and Kathy Kirby all enjoyed Tommy's company and he theirs.

In Kathy's case he remembers wonderful fish and chip lunches spent in each other's company during their breaks on the 'Stars and Garters' show. He says in those days Kathy was a great conversationalist, discussing a variety of subjects and having lots of laughs. Most of this time was spent in the studio canteen because he and Kathy were so popular then they couldn't walk very far without being mobbed by fans. That being the case they would never have got back to carry on rehearsing or filming if they had gone out.

Lots of the girls who he met along the way were great company but it was clear to Tommy, that the lovely young singer Sheila Prytherch was something special. So he set out his stall to woo her and win her heart.

Sheila was one of the Vernon Girls, a stunningly attractive and vivacious girl from Liverpool with a fabulous voice and a wonderful sense of humour. Tommy couldn't stop thinking about her and they met again on a train travelling up from London to Manchester. Fresh from working in his job at Covent Garden market and still overawed by what was happening to him in the business and very shy, he got up the nerve to ask her out. He was sure she would say yes, because, he was known by his friends as *Tommy Sweet Talk* because the man who gave him this name,

Troy Dante, better known as The Face was amazed by Tommy's natural charm. Troy, who hoped to rival Jess Conrad as the best looking man in show business, said Tommy, as shy as he was, could sweet talk all the girls into anything.

Interestingly Troy gave all the gang of friends at the time known as 'The Collection', nicknames. Andrew Ray was Larry The Lamb, Gordon Mills one of the Viscounts was called the Mule, The Gun from the Green was Mitch Murray, the well-known songwriter. We mustn't forget The Disneyland Prince, Jess Conrad all those of us who know and like Jess, smile at this nickname because we knew where Troy was coming from with this one.

However in Troy's case, 'The Face' as good-looking as Troy was and I am sure still is, was merely a pseudonym for another part of his anatomy according to his friends, donkey face was what they called him. Best I leave it there I think.

Of course the other connection between Tommy Sweet Talk and The Face was Barry Mason who managed them both at the time. After being introduced to each other by Shirley Ann Field, Barry let Troy make a demonstration disc of a song he had written aptly named *The Face.* Interestingly Tommy sang backing vocals on the disc in a deep bass voice. Dick Rowe at Decca liked it and gave Troy a recording contract.

Tommy, Troy and Barry went on an ill-fated tour of Ireland together. This tour was organised by another friend Leapy Lee.

Lee would go on to have his own hit with '*Little Arrows*', incidentally the deal for the record was partly brokered by Troy showing yet again the recurring links in show business. The tour was a complete disaster and the least said about it the better, even though as usual the lads managed to have a good time. Leapy Lee would also go on to have his much publicised problems with the law due to his friendship with Diana Dors and Alan Lake. Troy Dante was involved with Dors for five years and it was he who introduced Lee to them.

Tommy has often wondered what happened to Troy who he thinks went over to America to try his luck there for a while. Recent information suggests that Troy is living in Blackpool. In the interest of hearing his memories I will try and contact him as I have done with others who have been friends of Tommy's over the years.

To go back to the story Sheila who tells me she was travelling with her friend Sally said, 'well I couldn't possibly go without my friend as we always stay together', so Tommy had to take them both to dinner. However Tommy and Sheila were rapidly falling in love and there would be other opportunities for them to spend time alone together.

Big things were happening and one of the men at the forefront of the British popular music scene was Larry Parnes. He soon realised that Tommy was something special and even though he was not one of the Parnes boys as such, not having been discovered by him. Larry had no hesitation in featuring him on the sixteen week 'Rock and Trad Spectacular' tour.

This was a mammoth undertaking by Parnes, the show did full weeks at places like the Liverpool Empire and the Newcastle Empire with one night stands in between. Being on the road for that amount of time is really exhausting Tommy and the others looked on the residencies as a rest!

Of course there were laughs along the way, Dave Sampson recalls, when they did a week in Manchester, it rained all the time. Tommy, Dave and Nelly, (Nelson Keene) who became Tommy's great friend and who he still misses today, sat in the hotel all week eating fierce ruby's, with the natural result. As he said never mind the sex and drugs that go with rock and roll all they got were sore arses.

Another time they booked into a hotel and the boys were asked what their breakfast requirements would be for the week. Most of them asked for full English and the *Daily Mirror*, but Dickie Pride said a bottle of scotch and *The Daily Worker*. The manager nearly choked. Especially when Dave Sampson added you might forget the paper mate but you do not want to be around if you forget the scotch.

There were so many acts on that tour they had to use three coaches, one for the band, there were sixteen musicians, one for the boys and a separate one for the Vernon girls there were sixteen of them as well, all chaperoned. Vernon's football pools were behind the girls and they insisted on them being chaperoned. Tommy has wonderful memories of the tour and the people involved in it. One man who might well have been involved in this tour as assistant to Rita Gillespie on the second leg was Alan Wheeler, had it not being for the fact that his £5 wage was thirty bob less than he was getting as a messenger.

He decided he would stick with his job as messenger and carry on running Marty Wilde's fan club. Although he later regretted the decision not to work on the tour he did travel on the coach two or three times on each leg, taking the programmes. By doing this he got to know the guys quite well. So much so that he later managed Dickie Pride for a while.

Strangely enough while writing this book I received an email from a gentleman called Don Brandon. He was 84 years of age at the time of writing and he drove the Timpsons coach that carried the boys around the country to the gigs on the 'Rock and Trad' tour. He also booked ahead for the accommodation that was required in the various towns.

His memories of the tour include, as he puts it, Tommy's fabulous rendition of Freddy Cannon's great number *'Way Down Yonder In New Orleans'*, Incidentally Tommy has fond memories of touring the UK with Freddy when he first came over here. He remembers him as a lovely guy and became friendly with him. Also he has often said that Freddy is a real Rock'n'Roller an accolade Tommy doesn't hand out very often, always giving a performance full of bounce and energy that draws the audience to him. An interesting comparison in both their performances because unlike many artistes both Tommy and Freddy like to have the house lights up so that they can talk to and see the audience. Making each performance as Tommy puts it feel like a night out with friends.

Interestingly I talked to Freddy when he toured with 'The Solid Gold Sixties Show' last year, and he expressed fond memories of Tommy. Saying that he thought he would always be a success with live audiences because they feel that Tommy is just like them and in spite of the glitz and the glamour surrounding him as a performer he is just like one of their mates when he talks to them. Once again showing that Tommy is just the same as he has always been, the boy from Covent Garden Market. As did Bobby Vee on each of the occasions I have been in his company. He was another of the American stars that Tommy had the pleasure of spending time with, of course they had a connection through the record company, due to Norrie Paramour working on recording sessions with him when Bobby was in England, around about 1963. In fact Bobby left Tommy a photograph with a wonderful personal message attached.

Others on the show included Eddie Cochrane during a very brief spell in the weeks around the time *Ain't Misbehavin'* was released, Eddie actually died in a car crash just outside Chippenham. Tommy remembers Eddie as a perfect gentleman. Tommy often stood in for and also worked with Gene Vincent who, he remembers was an exciting guy to be around, he recalls the habit Gene had of hitting his bad leg and saying things like, 'keep going Henry'.

Of course no-one can get on with everyone and in Tommy's case the big American star he toured with on one occasion had reason to know that, when push comes to shove, Tommy Bruce takes no prisoners. The star in question was none other than The Killer himself Jerry Lee Lewis. Tommy says that Jerry Lee was absolute dynamite a tremendous performer and that it was a terrific honour to perform on the shows with him.

However it seems that The Killer told the compère that he thought Tommy Bruce was doing too well so he had to be brought off stage early in future. When the compère passed this message on to Tommy he just growled in his gravel voice that unless the pair of them were cruising for a bruising things would be left as they were. The message seemed to get through, as there was no change to Tommy's spot.

Others appearing on that tour in 1962 were The Alisons, The Bachelors, Danny Storme, Mark Eden who would later become the sinister Alan Bradley in Coronation Street and Dave Reid and the Echoes. Once again a tremendous line up put together by a man who would come back again to haunt me - the legendary Don Arden.

We cannot leave Tommy's memories of the American stars without mentioning Peggy Lee. Tommy remembers meeting her at EMI headquarters before they recorded a show together. The show was called 'Monday Spectacular' and for Tommy it was a real thrill to perform with such a massive star.

As he said it really showed just how far his lucky star had risen. Tommy says Peggy Lee was absolutely gorgeous, unbelievably sexy with a warm personality and as he added what a voice. Of course Tommy Sweet Talk, ever the gallant gentleman kissed her hand, something he was prone to do with the ladies, Helen Shapiro was another to receive this attention.

Another of Don Brandon's more personal memories of Tommy is of the night that there was a problem with the advance booking arrangements. Having booked accommodation for everyone including himself, they arrived in Huddersfield to find they were one room short. He resigned himself to an uncomfortable night on the coach only to be surprised by an offer from Tommy to bunk in with him.

Tommy remembers this incident and said, 'for a boy who'd been in the orphanage and the army it was no hardship just the right thing to do'. For Don however as he sits at home now in Guilford, Surrey, it is a wonderful memory of the exciting times he spent with some of this countries most exciting young talent.

The tour was a great opportunity for Tommy and the other young stars; they would learn a lot from having the support of great musicians backing them. Tommy remembers the talents of guys like The Jimmy Nicolls Big Band, Eric Ford - guitar, Red Price, John Hawksworth - bass guitar, Sid Dale, Colin Green - guitar and Benny Green are some of the names that Tommy remembers.

Incidentally Colin Green went on to be Shirley Bassey's musical director. These guys showed all the boys including Tommy the professionalism that would be needed to succeed in the business.

Tommy can still feel the excitement at the opening of the show as the band started to play the *Mardi Gras March* and the Vernon Girls would come in from the back of the theatre and dance their way through the audience and down to the stage. It was a wonderful opening full of noise, colour and excitement, reminiscent of a New Orleans carnival atmosphere. Of course everything was new and Larry Parnes was full of ideas to make the show have an impact.

Mind you one of Larry's ideas did not go down too well with Billy. Larry thought it would be a good thing if all the boys came in from the back of the auditorium along with girls. All very nice in theory but as Billy said, when it was put into practice, 'we are getting ripped to pieces by the fans on the way out, do you want them to kill us before we get in?'

Larry, astute and ruthless businessman that he was, did not want the merchandise ruined before the performance so he scrapped that plan. He had plenty of other ideas to make the show go with a bang.

Quick changes were the order of the day, with no time to get back to the dressing room. Starting the show in red blazer and boater Tommy for example would have to get in to a leopard skin and carry a club for a performance with Lynn Cornell from the Vernon Girls similarly attired.

In the course of all the changes the guys and the Vernon Girls would frequently find themselves naked back stage all at the same time. But as Tommy says you hardly noticed because you only had two or three minutes till whoever was on stage finished their number and then you had to be ready to run back on the green to do your thing.

There may not have been time to go back to the dressing room but the whole show from an audience point of view was very professional and slick. Lessons learnt on that tour have been standing Tommy in good stead throughout his whole career. Parnes was like Jack Good a hard taskmaster but if you wanted to have a good act and present yourself well in the business, you would be glad in later years that you listened to both of them.

Of course Larry Parnes's ideas were all about making a profit. He had a huge outlay in terms of travel costs and hotel accommodation; the whole thing was run like a military operation. Although the boys were becoming famous the wages were not great and many of them, including Billy and Dickie, were often short of money.

Tommy because his money came via Barry and Norrie, and Dave Sampson who was paid by his manager Tito Burns, were on a different pay scale, although they did not know it then. They just thought the other boys were spending faster than them and would often lend them five or ten bob (shillings) to keep them going, as Tommy has said it was like a family and families help each other.

Tommy's second record release *'Broken Doll'* coincided with the start of the tour so Larry came up with the idea that Tommy should take a toy doll on stage and tear it to pieces during his performance of the song. As the newspapers reported at the time, Tommy objected strongly to this, reaching a point where he refused to discuss it anymore and stormed off. He locked himself in the dressing room for an hour, but in the end Parnes got his way. As Tommy said afterwards, 'in the end Larry Parnes was the governor and you just had to do what he said.'

When Tommy did as Larry had said the girls screamed and

shouted and by the end of the song, when he would throw the doll's head into the audience, some had been known to faint from the self generated hysteria.

Billy Fury became a great friend; one of the nicest, quietest guys Tommy ever met, very laid back but on stage he was dynamite! Unfortunately even in those days Billy had trouble with his health and he had to miss a few dates during the tour.

On two occasions Billy nearly made himself unavailable for the rest of the tour, by insisting he would drive himself to the gigs instead of riding on the coach. On one of these occasions he crashed his new MG sports car banging his head and shaking himself up quite badly. He did quite a bit of damage to the car including bending the steering wheel.

He asked Tommy to drive him to the next show, which happened to be in Liverpool, Billy's hometown. Tommy agreed but it was a nightmare journey with the steering wheel bent to hell causing Tommy to arrive in Liverpool with backache, neck ache and 'every other bloomin' ache.' Billy just laughed at Tommy's complaints, after all what are friends for, if not to suffer for you.

A regular visitor to Billy's family home, Tommy was well liked particularly by Billy's brother Albie, who often recalls, on one occasion, Tommy being asleep in the car outside the house. On this visit Albie, who thought a lot of Tommy then and still does, was looking all over the house for him and shouting to his mam,

'Tommy's here I know he is.'

'Well where is he?' Asked Jean.

'Well his car's outside,' said Albie, 'so he must be somewhere.'

Eventually after searching for some time he found Tommy asleep in the car.

Incidentally under the name of Jason Eddie, Albie would have some success in show business himself. He still performs tribute shows to his brother on a regular basis under the auspices of his manager and promoter Chris Hewitt. Albie is one of the good guys and he has worked tirelessly with his mum the lovely Jean to take care of Billy's fans and make sure that everyone remembers Billy for the right reasons.

One of Billy's biggest problems always came at the end of every show, a couple of hundred girls would be waiting at the stage door screaming their heads off and fainting and Billy found it difficult in the melee to reach the coach and the physical effort always drained him. It was plain even in those days that his health was not as robust as it might have been.

An even more serious incident for Billy took place after one of the shows. After his performance had ended in Portsmouth Billy decided to take a walk along the shore to get some air. While walking he slipped and hit his head on the rocks. Sometime later Tommy and Nelson Keene together as always, following the same route saw something bobbing in the water.

Realising it was a person, Tommy jumped in and grabbed hold of the body, it was only as Nelly helped pull him out they realised it was Billy. Billy's career could have ended before it really began if not for Tommy and Nelly's timely arrival, this incident only served to strengthen the boys' existing friendship.

Nelly remembers another time when Billy was singing a song about the best man in town. Some of the local lads took it to heart and when Billy left the theatre they set about him. What they didn't know was that next out of the door was Tommy Bruce and seeing what was happening to Billy, Tommy took no prisoners and he really sorted them out.

As Nelly said they were left in no doubt as to who really was the best man in town. It seems to be from many reports given by Tommy's friends that he was perceived as a tough guy and very often a few well chosen words would be enough to put a stop to any lads who wanted to cause trouble.

Billy Fury, Tommy,
Joe Brown and
Jack Good

Tommy and Nelly

All the Gang

Tommy, Eden Kane
and Billy Fury

Albert, fan, Tommy
and Mildred

Tommy and Sheila's
Wedding Day

Albert and Tommy
with Tommy Jnr

The unique style and gravel-edged voice of Tommy Bruce could not be more adequately expressed than in the 1963 rendition of *Lavender Blue* (Columbia Records), that entered the British charts selling over a million copies. However, before the gold disc of *Lavender Blue* could be presented to Tommy, it disappeared from the wall of Columbia Studios and remained missing for many years. It is typical of the thoughtful nature of Dave Lodge, that he should have spent so much time and trouble in tracking down the missing disc to give to Tommy.

I was pleased and very honoured to present the disc to Tommy on Dave's behalf (although forty years too late!!) at the Butlins' Rock'n'Roll Festival of 2004. That Gold Record is now, to me, a fitting tribute to both Tommy Bruce and the man he calls "The brother I didn't have". They are simply two of the nicest gentlemen and you cannot say better than that.

Frank Godfrey
Oldies But Goodies
Dec. 2005

Sitting in Norrie Paramour's, my recording manager's office one afternoon in early 1960, going through demos with him, as I was about to cut my second record for Columbia/EMI. He suddenly got up out of his chair and went over to the hi-fi and placed a record on the turntable and said to me what do you think of this Dave?

Well at the end of two and a half minutes of playing time I just sat there gobsmacked and speechless. When I recovered I asked, 'Who was that?'

Norrie replied, 'it's a new guy I just signed, his name is Tommy Bruce.'

I had never heard a voice like his in my life it was like someone shoveling gravel in tune and it was so different that in 1960 it just had to be a massive hit.

As you all know that is exactly what it was, '*Ain't Misbehavin*' went straight to the top of the NME charts and the rest is pop history.

Four months later we were together on tour in Larry Parnes 'Rock And Trad Spectacular with our good pals Billy Fury, Joe Brown, Georgie Fame etc, and began friendships that have lasted to this day. We became touring roommates along with our other great pal Nelly (Nelson Keene) and enjoyed many laughs together on the road.

I am sure that Dave will have told you a few of those in the book but will just add one more in case he hasn't. Tommy always looked immaculate and his pride and joy was his barnet (hair), it was a mass of curls and always looked the 'business'. On this one occasion we had arrived on the tour bus to do a show in Cheltenham, usually we got a friendly reception from the fans and public in general. This night it was different, there were a few likely lads hanging about and as I got off the bus right behind Tommy who hadn't walked three yards before one lad ran up and messed Tommy's hair up. WRONG MOVE! Tommy who was always very placid picked the guy up and in his best Stepney accent shouted 'Do that agin an oi'll eatcha' then put him down. The kid was gone in a flash not to be seen again.

Now about my friend Tommy who would rather eat Pie 'n' Mash in Manzies than eat in a flash restaurant, who would sooner go for an evening of Bingo than go to a night club and who would sooner drink a pint of Guinness than a glass of Champagne… what does that tell you? It tells you that Tommy Bruce who is an Eastender just like me has not changed one iota in all his 46 years in Showbiz… There are many I could name who forget that you, the reader of this book and the record buying members of the public and the fans who still come to their concerts to this day, made them all a success in the beginning. Tommy has never forgotten those people in all the 46 years I have known him. He has never refused to sign an autograph or pose for a photograph. He never bad mouths anyone or puts him or her down.

Tommy you are one in a million a very special friend and I feel honoured to have been asked by Dave to write this tribute for his book on your great life. You have always made me smile and you know everyone on this Great British Rock'n' Roll circle loves you. Do you know something mate? Even to this day there has never been anyone with a 'Obsons like yours…. To quote a phrase…. ROCK ON TOMMY!!! Luv U Mate!

Dave Sampson
Columbia Recording artiste.

Chapter Twelve

The thing that shows through while researching this book is that if Tommy Bruce thinks you are his friend he will stand up and look after you in whatever way he feels necessary, regardless of what might happen to him. I know this to be true because in different ways Tommy has always looked after me. I think that his upbringing and his experiences in the orphanage have moulded a very fine, considerate and complex man. The only problem with this is that he gives so freely of himself he expects the same loyalty and caring in return. Not everybody can be so selfless and as the years have gone by some of the people Tommy cared about have disappointed him by just living a different life. They did this not knowing the effect this would have on Tommy and his perception of what they thought of him. That said those of us truly blessed with his friendship would not have him any other way.

Another good mate of Tommy's was Dickie Pride, The Sheik Of Shake, as he was dubbed. He was the total opposite of Billy, loud and brash somehow always finding trouble as Tommy says albeit with great affection, Dickie could best be described as a bit of a nutter.

A great entertainer, the girls loved him and the way he would start to shake from his ankles until his whole body was going, was amazing. Dickie should have been one of this country's greatest entertainers in Tommy's opinion and yet he had to drive a truck at one stage to make a living. But fate and, what in Dickie's opinion, was poor management decisions about the material he recorded, conspired to make Dickie very unhappy about most of the aspects of his career. The same could be said about many of the talented boys who tried to make their careers in the rock and roll era. Incidentally Dickie was another of the boys who courted a Vernon girl, Maureen Kennedy, but sadly in his case she was tragically killed in a car crash, while protecting her baby with her own body on what in those days was a very new motorway; the M1.

Jess Conrad had reason to appreciate Dickie's talent as the recording studio always phoned Dickie before having Jess in to make a record, as Dickie always sang the high notes. However anyone who thought with Dickie's demise that Jess's career would end were sadly mistaken as Jess has remained a star in a career that spans nearly fifty years. He is also one of Tommy's and my, best friends in the business.

Joe Brown was another who Tommy liked and admired. He was and is a great guitarist; fantastic to work with and he always had loads of ideas about how he wanted his career and his music to progress. Along with Marty, Joe is one of the highest paid artistes from the sixties still performing today. Also like Marty, Joe's daughter, Sam, has had chart success. Incidentally like Tommy, Marty and Joe married Vernon's Girls.

Marty *The Big M* as Tommy has always called him, was a huge star in the UK, even Cliff Richard has been heard to say he thought if one person would go on to have one of the biggest careers in the music industry it would be Marty. Undaunted by setbacks along the way Marty has established himself as a big box office draw on the sixties revival scene as well as being a successful songwriter. He has also seen his daughter, Kim, have great success.

Danny Rivers a good-looking dark haired boy with a great voice was another in the Parnes stable. Also very popular with the ladies it seemed for a while as though Danny would be one of the lasting successes from the stable, however in spite of going on to tour with American stars like Johnny Burnette, Gene McDaniels, Gary US Bonds and also singing with the Cyril Stapleton Orchestra he just slipped from the limelight.

Danny's lack of real success in the charts was surprising but also contributed to his career at the top of the entertainment ladder not happening. That said Danny, in the company of his wife Emily, is a popular addition to many of the sixties weekends that are put on around the UK. Indeed Robert Plant, in a recent interview on the excellent Susie Quatro's radio show said that three of the best singers and performers around in his favourite era of music the early sixties, were Billy Fury, Vince Eager and Danny Rivers. Thus proving that Danny is, in the minds of many people, a sixties icon and is without doubt an important part of the sixties music scene.

The list goes on, Tommy's close friend Dave Sampson a singer with a great voice struggled with comparisons to Cliff Richard, something he has had to endure, even to this day. Anyone who has heard Dave sing knows there is far more to him than just sounding like Cliff Richard. He is a great performer in his own right and deserves to be remembered for his own achievements. To this very day Dave continues to receive plaudits about his voice from such luminaries as James Burton the legendary guitarist who played with Ricky Nelson and Elvis Presley. It is so difficult to understand how Dave has not managed to have more recognition throughout the business.

Duffy Power was very popular with the fans back then, Johnny Gentle as Tommy says; gentle by name and nature, Lance Fortune who Tommy always thought was a real talent, and Peter Wynne who he remembers as a very nice guy with a great voice. Another who Tommy remembers as being a lovely boy was Cuddly Dudley, he often wonders what happened to him. Not forgetting the previously mentioned Big M, Marty Wilde, we have to say there is no doubt he was something else and all the girls were crazy about him.

Nelson Keene had covered Bobby Vee's *'Rubber Ball'* and recently released *'Image of a Girl'* and *'Ocean of Love'* on the HMV label and so Larry Parnes decided he should join the tour. Nelly and Tommy had already hit it off becoming great friends when they appeared in summer season at the Queens Theatre Blackpool, during the 'Idols on Parade' show, so this gave them the opportunity to strengthen their friendship. They did everything together horse riding, trips out, with girls or maybe just to look for a couple. As Nelly said in an interview once during the Rock and Trad tour, Tommy is the guy who helps me out when I get in trouble. Tommy would often stay at Nelly's sister Kath's house and became a close friend of the family.

Also part of the team was Nelly's brother Roy who used to chauffeur the boys around and tease Tommy about the songs he sang. Tommy used to say to Nelly 'don't let that brother of yours sit in the front row or I won't be able to do my act'. Of course we should not forget to mention a man who had no official connection with the tour but joined in all the fun. Travelling in his Rolls Royce and up for anything Robin Ashton-Jones, he has never been heard of since but Tommy says he was a great guy.

Great days and great fun as Tommy said it seemed it would never end. There never seemed to be time for sleep as the next exciting chapter of events was just waiting to be lived. Tommy often says to me he wishes Nelly would come back from Australia just once so they could relive the happy memories that they share.

Billy Raymond, Georgie Fame (who would have even greater success later in his career), Johnny Goode, Lyn Cornell who Tommy used to chase across the stage dressed in a leopard skin armed with a club, much to the delight of the screaming girls in the audience and The Viscounts. There were so many of them and the strange thing was there was no rivalry, Tommy felt he was part of one big happy family. There has never been anything remotely like the Rock and Trad show since those days. There is no doubt that Larry Parnes was one of the great innovators of his generation and kick started some great careers.

One of Tommy's other friends who he used to go riding within the company of Garth Kaywood, Vince Eager and Nelson Keene was Michael Cox hit recording star of *'Angela Jones'* fame. Michael and Tommy kept company often during the sixties and as Tommy says had a great time. They lost touch when Michael emigrated to New Zealand in 1975 and Tommy has not heard from him in many years.

There are other people who became Tommy's friends and remained so. Two of them are Mike Berry and John Leyton. Mike seems to have always been there but John was away due to his acting career. However Tommy and I are delighted to say he is around more and more in recent times.

Mike is always good to be around and when needed can be relied upon. He and Tommy have often appeared together over the years. He has had great success as a television actor to add to what he has achieved as a singer. He has appeared in series like *Are You Being Served* and *Wurzel Gummage*. Mike has also achieved recognition in America. Indeed latest news from Mike is that he has just recorded a new CD album with The Crickets, showing that he continues to be just as popular and in demand as ever.

Mike said one of the nicest things anyone has ever said about Tommy to me was when he said that 'there was nothing show business about Tommy, he was just the same genuine lad that first came off the market and into the business.'

Tommy remembers that he and John Leyton worked together for the first time at the Colston Halls in Bristol. Tommy thought John was a really nice guy, and remembers that he was very nervous because it was his first appearance as a singer, up to that point he had been an actor. The show was called 'We're No Squares'.

The Charles Blackwell Orchestra provided the backing for the boys and guess who was on drums that night? Our great friend, the wonderful Clem Cattinni. It's funny how the same people turn up over and over again throughout Tommy's life and for the most part these are the people who mattered most to him.

Robert Stigwood was John's manager at this time and this was his first musical production and apart from Tommy and John it had Michael Medwin, famous at that time for his role as Corporal Springer in the television series *The Army Game* as the compère.

It is strange how the links to people and events continue to appear throughout Tommy's career. Bernard Breslaw who also starred in *The Army Game* would go on to make a film about national service in the army and Tommy sang the theme song to it, the song was entitled *'Two Left Feet'*.

Tommy and John worked together on a few occasions, including lengthy summer seasons as promoters, you could see there was a good rapport and balance of performance between the two entertainers. However, it wasn't too long before John's obvious talent as an actor took his career in that direction.

Tommy didn't see John for about thirty years, until the 'Telstar Tour' show at the Beck Theatre, due to the fact that John had an outstandingly successful career in Hollywood. Tommy was pleased that John came back on the circuit and is always delighted to be in his company.

Strangely enough that was John's theatre comeback show as a singer and once again Tommy was there. I was the compère on that night and met John for the first time and remember how nervous he was. I told him he had no need to be, as soon as he went on stage the audience loved him and welcomed him back as if he had never been gone.

John is a wonderful actor and the list of his film credits is endless, two of his great and best remembered films are *The Great Escape* and *Von Ryan's Express*. He still has a good following with the fans and they always look forward to his concerts. His songs *'Johnny Remember Me'* and *'Son This Is She'* are still in great demand.

Mike and John are both always remembered for their association with the now legendary Joe Meek, as are many of our other friends, some no longer with us like Heinz and Screamin' Lord Sutch. Dave Sutch although a quiet man in everyday life was dynamite on stage.

Tommy and I remember wild performances when Screamin' would set the venue's carpets alight as he performed his cult song *'Jack the Ripper'*. He would come on stage whirling a lit brazier around with sparks and coals flying everywhere, holding the severed head of one of the female victims in his other hand. Then whoever had been elected to be the policeman, Larry (The Teapot) Richards was one who had the job on a few occasions and sometimes it would be a fan who was known to us. I did it now and then and I still have the damaged knuckles to prove it, because part of the unsuccessful bid to capture Jack, (Screamin'), involved a hectic sword fight. That would have been okay but there was only one metal sword and Screamin' always had that, leaving the likes of me with a piece of wood, resulting in powerful blows from Screamin' striking our unprotected hands.

That said there is no doubt that Dave Sutch along with Jess Conrad was one of the finest self-publicists ever. Also some of his political ideas, expounded through his Monster Raving Loony Party, although rubbished at the time, somehow later found their way into other party's manifestos. He was championing the voting age to be reduced to eighteen long before anyone else.

Tommy and Jess were often out and about on the campaign trail with him and they always had a good time together. Although he could be irritating with his bad time-keeping and tendency to moan about the slightest thing, we loved him, he was a great guy and a good friend we were blessed to have him in our lives.

Another thing that continues the associations theme is the fact that while John and Robert Stigwood were making a promotional tour they found the song *'Tell Him'* for our other friend the lovely Billie Davis. It is strange how the links between the artistes continue because of course, both Billie and Graham Fenton recorded for the Magnet record label.

Of course we must not forget Vince Eager at this point in the book. He was another who came under the auspices of Larry Parnes and Jack Good. After Vince had been with his own band, the Vagabonds, Larry saw the tall good-looking Vince as a solo artiste of the highest calibre and in his live performances he certainly came well up to expectations. That said chart success eluded him, it maybe that Larry Parnes was already heavily involved with promoting Marty Wilde and may have felt a conflict of interests, many people thought then, and still do, that Vince should have had a hit recording. However Vince's television career went from strength to strength being one of the star attractions along with Adam Faith on 'DrumBeat'. Vince was often called upon by Larry Parnes to act as his representative on some of the road shows that were out at the time. For many years Vince has been on the cruise ships and he also appeared extensively abroad. Many people, including Tommy, are very pleased to see him back on the circuit in the UK where he is still a very popular artiste, appearing up and down the country to rave reviews.

Vince put out his own very successful show 'Raised on Rock' and Wee Willie Harris, Liquorice Locking, of Shadows fame and Big Jim Sullivan, who incidentally played that wonderful solo on Tommy's hit *'Lavender Blue'* appeared with him. Tommy did a very successful three-night stint with Vince in Grantham. Once again Tommy has said that Vince is someone for whom he has high regard.

It is impossible to mention Tommy's friends without recalling Chas McDevitt; Chas is, in Tommy's opinion, one of the country's finest talents. One time king of skiffle, a former King Rat and more importantly a really nice guy who has the respect of us all,

Chas McDevitt is an important part of British musical history.

Some of the boys did not stay in the business like Cuddley Dudley, Davy Jones and also it would seem Peter Wynn. Tommy has not heard of any of these lads for years; some of the others who did keep performing did not have the same success as Tommy, Billy, Marty and Joe. In spite of that they were all an important part of that special time in the early sixties when it seemed that all things were possible in the entertainment world.

For Tommy the gigs went on and he must have done hundreds of gigs with Billy Fury, including two very long summer seasons one in Great Yarmouth and one in Blackpool. Tommy also did summer seasons in Blackpool with Joe Brown and John Leyton, he never tired of Billy's company or his stage work.

During this time Billy's road manager was Hal Carter, Tommy got to know him very well and he would pop up often in his career, as the years went by, in his capacity as one of the country's most successful agents and promoters. The story goes that Hal joined a circus and among other things put his head in a lion's mouth. Tommy and I believe it, if that's what it was going to take to succeed, Hal would do it. He was a courageous and honourable man and his knowledge of the business was second to none.

During the course of the 'Rock and Trad' spectacular, in spite of the close attentions of the chaperone, Tommy courted Sheila and got to know her very well. He really thought she could be the one to settle down and spend his life with.

So she and Tommy were rapidly becoming an item and although it meant Sheila would miss out on the chance of a solo career, they married in 1964. This was a happy occasion, Sheila's friend Julie Sharpe who was, I believe, also her cousin was chief bridesmaid. Bobby Coral from the Bruisers stood as Tommy's best man.

The decision to put family life before her career was one Sheila did not regret when twelve months later in 1965 she gave birth to their son Tommy junior. Then in 1970 along came their lovely daughter Lorraine. It seemed then that life could not get any better.

Incidentally one of the many happy times Tommy spent with his children was during the summer season in Hastings, the year that Lorraine was born. Sheila brought Lorraine and young Tommy to spend the first week or so with Tom and then went home with the baby. Leaving young Tom to spend the summer with his dad.

Tommy recalls the kindness of an arcade attendant, who kept young T, as Tommy likes to call his son, well supplied with tokens. Tommy also likes to think that that summer helped create the loving bond that exists between father and son to this very day. Tommy is a very family orientated man whose love for both his children is immense.

Sheila's talent as a mother was even greater than her vocal talent, which is second to none, her love and care along with

Tommy's produced two talented and gifted children who are also two of the nicest people you could wish to meet.

Sheila and Tommy sang as a duo for a time, to considerable effect and success on the cabaret circuit Tommy looks back on this period as being one of his happiest in show business.

One of the other Vernons Girls is Maggie Stredder; she is the sexy one with the glasses who has been driving the lads wild from the very beginning, Tommy thinks the world of her. I spoke to her recently and believe me guys she is still a very sexy lady with a great personality.

You may remember Maggie in fairly recent times using her soaring voice to compliment John Leyton's in the performance of *'Johnny Remember Me'*, on the Solid Gold Sixties shows. Incidentally some of you may recall that Lisa Grey sang with him on the recording. Following the publication of her book, Maggie is much in demand to give talks on her time in the sixties music scene. She is very happily married these days to her husband Jim who for many years ran his own very successful entertainment agency.

Maggie is a very good friend of Tommy's and she will tell anyone who asks that Tommy was one of the most exciting performers to come out of the sixties. She remembers him as a very good-looking boy whose talent was so different it made him stand out from the rest. She thinks he is still an outstanding performer.

Another of the people from the sixties who Tommy came into contact with was the actor Dudley Sutton. Dudley appeared in the film '*The Boys*' with Jess Conrad and Richard Todd. He always thought well of Tommy. Tommy is always delighted to see Dud, in any of the many television productions he appears in these days. As he says, 'Dud is a talented, hard worker who deserves all the success he has had'.

Tommy has always made time for charity shows and right from the very start of his career he has given his support to anyone who has asked. In the early days he was often called upon by The Variety Club of Great Britain to attend fundraisers in the company of other artistes. He always remembers time in the company of Bruce Forsyth at these events as special moments in his career.

As far as Tommy is concerned Bruce Forsyth is the guvnor when it comes to entertainment. Way back in 1960 Tommy said that Bruce was the nicest guy he had met among the established stars in the business. A really great guy who helped him a lot, Tommy stood in the wings to watch him work on many occasions. There is nothing Bruce doesn't know about show business says Tommy who has no hesitation in saying Bruce Forsyth is simply the best. In Tommy's opinion and mine for what it's worth, if any entertainer ever deserved a knighthood it is Bruce and hopefully by the time this is book published he will have received one.

Another memorable occasion was a concert for The Stars Organisation for Spastics in 1961 at Wembley's Empire Pool. Tommy performed in a fabulous line-up that included, Joan Regan, Vera Lynn (the Chairman of the SOS), Alma Cogan, Eve Boswell, Matt Monroe, Gary Miller, and John Barry.

The performance took place in front of thirteen thousand people, the artistes all worked for no fee and all the proceeds went to the charity. It does us good to remember that long before Band-Aid our great stars were putting something back in for those less fortunate than themselves. Tommy appeared in many of these shows but this was made more memorable by the line up.

Tommy really loved Matt Monroe both as a person and as a performer, he thought he had a wonderful voice but more than that he was a really nice guy. Tommy recalls how close Matt was to leaving the business. He was on his way in to see Norrie one day and met Matt coming out of the studio. Matt was taking some records up to the BBC something that they all did from time to time; one of them was Tommy's new release *'Lavender Blue'*. Tommy greeted him in his own enthusiastic style.

'How's it going?' he asked Matt.

'Not too good,' Matt replied, 'if this *'Portrait of my Love'* thing doesn't do anything I'm going back to driving a bus. Unlike Tommy, who had achieved almost instant success due to being in the right place at the right time, although without his unique talent the opportunity would not have been of much use, something Tommy never forgets, that many other talented people struggled really hard for that initial recognition. As was the case for Matt, who in spite of his wonderful voice had spent years trying to become a success in the business and was understandably frustrated. Although as Tommy says in his opinion, Matt was such a determined guy there is no way he would ever have given up trying.

The rest is history; suffice it to say that Matt went on to have a great career and a much deserved place in the affections of all lovers of popular music. His legendary voice will be around as long as people listen to music.

Cuddley Dudley

Stills from the film:
The Man with the Yellow Hat

On the campaign trail with Dave Sutch

Vince Eager, Joe Brown, Jess Conrad, Tommy Bruce,
Albie Wycherley (Billy Fury's brother), Jean Wycherly (Billy's mum)

I first met Tom in the 1980s when he visited my home in Stockport for the first time with his manager, and my lifelong friend, Dave Lodge. Dave had frequently talked about his involvement with Tom and, as a fan of his sixties hits myself, I was delighted to meet the man with the gravel voice in person. Tom was living in Manchester at the time and I was pleased to be involved with some of the things that Dave was doing for Tom over the subsequent years.

Dave's relationship with Tom is more than that of just artist and manager, it is a close friendship bordering on brotherliness. On the professional side, the promotional work that Dave carries out for Tom is all consuming, to the exclusion of a number of other artists who would very much like Dave to promote them, but Dave remains loyal to Tom.

This book has been a true labour of love for Dave, often struggling through difficult personal circumstances to bring it to completion.

Needless to say, I have seen Tom perform live on many occasions and I am struck by the consummate professionalism displayed by him when he belts out the sixties classics. There is another side to Tom, though, and that is his ability to bring about a complete change of mood by giving a touching rendition of a ballad. He has real stage presence when he performs and he strikes up an instant rapport with his audience, making everyone feel as though he is relating to them personally.

On the personal side, Tom is not one of those stars who like to remain aloof from fans, he is always accessible, never forgetting that it was these people who made him the star he became. There is none of the celebrity attitude with Tom, he is a genuinely nice guy, and I wish him well for the future, hopefully returning to perform after his recent struggle with serious illness.

Peter Leonard

Although for many years I had heard about Tommy Bruce, the man with the gravel voice and big personality, I had never met him. That changed when I did a tribute dinner in honour of Billy Fury at the Adelphi Hotel in Liverpool and one of the most requested people I was asked to invite was Tommy Bruce. On that night a very quiet and shy man introduced himself as Tommy Bruce, he is the most lovely man you could wish to meet and so much wanted to be at this tribute to his great friend Billy Fury that he moved heaven and earth to be there, that's what I call a star!

I could not write anything about Tommy Bruce without mentioning the man who was responsible for Tommy Bruce being there that night, and who before the Billy Fury Tribute night I had never met, but only spoken to on the telephone, he is the author of this book Dave Lodge. I want to thank you Dave for becoming a wonderful friend to me since then, and for all the help and support you gave freely and selflessly to make sure that Tommy, and every other star from that era had a wonderful time. This book is long overdue, I cannot wait to read it.

Lyn Staunton
Power Promotions
Chairman of Northern the Variety Club of Great Britain

Chapter Thirteen

At this point we are slightly ahead of events, so we need to back track a little, variety shows were still popular in those days and in 1963 ATV decided that a weekly show set in a pub would appeal to the public.

The premise for the show was built on the idea of people being out for a drink and having a singsong. When Dorothy Shadwell saw Tommy on a late night TV show she knew straightaway that he was the type of act they needed for the show. So in conjunction with John Hamilton the decision was made to cast Tommy for that show.

The show was 'Stars and Garters' and at first in order to bring reality to the proceedings it was thought to be a good idea to bring the general public into the studio, yes it was filmed in a studio and not in a real pub as many people thought at the time. However it was soon seen that it was difficult for the general public to look as if they were having a good time while drinking weak cordial and not beer in a pub environment so that part of the idea was changed.

Incidentally Dorothy Shadwell had been partly responsible for the then young actor Jess Conrad coming into the music business.

When she cast him as Barney Day in ATV's 'Play for Today' *Bye Bye Barney* about a young rock and roll singer.

Interestingly Jess didn't sing during this play, Gary Mills provided vocals another success story from the sixties. Many fans best remember him for his recording of the lovely theme song from the film *Theatre of Horrors* starring Anton Differing, *'Look For A Star'*.

Of course Tommy was in great demand and promoters always wanted him as part of their shows, so when in 1962 a tour was set up for B. Bumble and The Stingers, Tommy was a must to be out there with them. He remembers the tour being great fun and once again, as was normally the case, found B. Bumble a good act to work with.

This tour gave him the chance once again to work with old friends Vince Eager and Johnny Kidd and the Pirates. Also appearing on the show were master guitarist Bert Weedon who Tommy still rates very highly on his list of all time great musicians, and Michael Cox whose memorable hit *'Angela Jones'* made him a real wow with the girls. Bert Weedon is still performing today. Michael Cox was last heard of living in New Zealand.

Then of course there was the fabulous 'Star Spangled Nights' tour, which saw Tommy appearing with a fantastic line up of stars. The line up had Don Munday as compère and included Tommy, Billy Fury, Joe Brown, Don Paul, Gordon Mills, Peter Jay, The

Alisons, The Viscounts, Peter Jay, Terry Hale and Karl Denver, who like Tommy had the most unique voice and sang the most wonderful songs.

Eden Kane recorded one of the great songs that Norrie Paramour had turned down for Tommy after he had been performing it for months. Tommy was getting great audience appreciation with *'Forget Me Not'* but Norrie said it couldn't be a hit. That along with *'I Like It'* which Tommy sang all through a summer season to rave reviews, long before Gerry Marsden sang it. They might have been big hits for Tommy if Norrie had taken a different view. However Norrie would just shrug and say, 'well, I can't be right all the time'. That said Tommy liked Eden and was pleased to perform with him again at the London Palladium in 2002.

'Star Spangled Nights' had a truly amazing line up not uncommon in its day but who could afford to put on anything to rival it today? Only the big charity shows where the artistes give their services free have anything like these line-ups.

Returning to 'Stars and Garters' this would be the show that changed everything for so many people including Tommy. It was actually inspired by another show called the Jubilee show. It had been hoped that the Jubilee with its old time larks in the pub would be ITV's answer to the BBC's hit show 'The Good Old Days' but it lacked something and didn't last. But the idea was deemed to be sound by the powers-that-be and so it proved with the new format, becoming the most popular variety show ITV had ever produced.

The new show starred Kathy Kirby, Tommy Bruce, Vince Hill and Clinton Ford, singer/songwriter Al Saxon. The show was introduced by mine host Ray Martine. That great vocal entertainer Kim Cordell would join them in the second series.

This show was a resounding success being the first programme to knock 'Coronation Street' off the top of the rating and voted The Best TV Series of 1963/1964 by national weekly magazine *Weekend*. Tommy Bruce was chosen to accept the award on behalf of everyone involved in the show.

A one off special was put on to mark the occasion, with Tommy being filmed receiving the award, in the shape of an eight-pointed star. This show did all the artistes' careers the power of good and made Tommy a household name. The powers-that-be are now putting similarly shaped stars down on the pavement in Covent Garden to recognise the achievements of various entertainers.

It is amazing that whatever the merits of the artistes chosen for this honour, Tommy Bruce's achievement as the local boy who came out of the area to become an internationally acclaimed artiste have not been recognised. It is something I will be working on with a view to redressing the balance in Tommy's favour.

Of course Tommy and Kathy Kirby developed a special

relationship during their time on the show, that in some ways continues to this day. Although Kathy is now a virtual recluse, the obvious affection Tommy has for her is apparent in the way he speaks of her. Kathy was a wonderful singer, who apart from having a great voice had fabulous personality and as he says 'a knockout to look at'. She really seemed to have been born to be a star.

When Kathy heard that Tommy was ill, although reluctant to leave her flat, because of her apprehension about being outside, she sent Tommy a lovely card and made an emotional phone call to him to offer him her good wishes for a return to health.

Vince Hill another important member of the cast with a wonderful voice was and still is respected by Tommy for his talent and professionalism. Of course Vince went on to have his own hits including the unforgettable *'Edelweiss'*. He is as popular today with his fans as he was in the sixties. He is also a very charming man with a great personality.

Clinton Ford will always be remembered for his great rendition of *'Fanlight Fanny'*, again I have to say that Clinton is a perfect gentleman and his continued success is testament to his talent and versatility. Anyone who has heard as I have, his performance of *'My Friend'* cannot fail to have been inspired by it. Recently I hear that Clinton has not been too well, Tommy and I wish him good health in the future.

Life for Tommy, as he sang in one of the shows, really seemed to be a bowl of cherries at this time. 'Stars and Garters' was performed as the summer season show at Lowestoft and was a great success.

Redifusion Television tried to repeat the format of the show with a new line up which included Susan Maughan. In spite of Susan's undoubted personality and talent something was missing and so one of the most popular shows in television history came to an end.

'Stars and Garters' had given Tommy the opportunity to show that whilst he would always be a rock and roller there was much more to his talent, he is an able dancer, very gifted musically with what can only be described as an infectious sense of humour, in fact he had the ability to be the complete all round entertainer, something that has stood him in good stead over the years, during times when there has been a temporary lull in his rock and roll bookings. Unlike many of his contempories whose careers stalled with the advent of the Beatles, Tommy has always been in great demand as a cabaret artiste, singing the old standards like *'Ramblin' Rose'*, *'Sweet Lorraine'* and *'Always'*.

The only downside to Tommy's contract with 'Stars and Garters' was that Barry Mason who had been with Tommy from the beginning decided that now would be a good time to go and pursue the song-writing career that was his ambition, working on the basis that he had taken Tommy as far as he could.

Tommy is a very affectionate man who gives his friendship and loyalty wholeheartedly, so when Barry left him he was heartbroken. He thought that show business was something they would always do together. So although he wished Barry luck it would be more than forty years before they spoke again.

It should be said that Barry was unaware of the effect his departure was to have on Tommy, as he had never made any secret of the fact that his ambitions lay in writing and performing himself. He never really considered himself a manager, because of this he did find the business side of personal management very tiring and by the time the split came he felt mentally drained.

Another thing that Tommy wondered about was the fact that as soon as Barry left him, the hit songs that Barry penned were coming thick and fast, not the least of them being recorded by Tom Jones. As Barry says there was no way of knowing the songs would be hits and when they were, it still didn't mean they would have worked for Tommy.

Barry also added somewhat cryptically that Gordon Mills, as the manager of Tom Jones was pretty hard line. We can draw any conclusion we like from that, but it would seem that it might not have always been Barry's decision as to who would record his songs. Barry still has great affection for Tommy and thinks fondly of the time they spent together.

At this point although the hit records were not coming it seemed that all the other aspects of Tommy's career were being given the Midas touch. Apart from the obvious music shows he was appearing in, there were many, from Tommy's point of view, surprising spin offs.

Diverse jobs like television adverts were coming his way one notable example was a voice over for the Quality Street Gang. This was an advert where all the chocolates in a box were given characters, like the one that Tommy remembers for a hard centre, that of an East End gangster, he was in his element with that. Tom voiced all the chocolates.

Another interesting job was the singing walrus in 'The Pinky and Perky Shows' a very popular children's show of the day. The walrus, being a puppet on strings, bounced about among others of his ilk, in a fish tank coming out from behind a rock with Tommy singing one of his recordings, *'Let's Do It (Let's Fall in Love')*. Great fun, it would probably be politically incorrect today.

One of the most surprising bookings Tommy received was the job of compère on a show he believes was called 'It's Mersey Beat'. All the great Liverpool groups of the day apart from the Beatles appeared, he remembers The Swinging Blue Jeans, The Fourmost and The Searchers.

Although chart success was eluding Tommy at this time, this booking shows his popularity with the fans and his pulling power as a live performer was such the promoters realised he was the man for the job. This recognition of his obvious personal pulling power is still clear today as promoters up and down the country still regard his presence as an enhancement to their shows.

One thing that Tommy recalls with great pleasure from his television days was meeting the now legendary producer Ernest Maxim. Ernest is unsurpassed in his skill for putting the right people in the right show in the right place at the right time. This is proved by his many awards from the industry, he has received Baftas, Golden Globes and a golden rose from the Montreax Festival.

Not bad for a boy who had been playing jazz piano in a minstrel show, only to be told at the age of nine, his career was over. Before becoming a television producer at twenty-two years of age he had an outstanding career as an actor, but then he really is a man of many talents. He was also highly lauded for his performance in a play called *The Golden Boy*, about a boxer who could play classical violin.

Going on to take the Marlon Brando role in an Australian production of a *Streetcar Named Desire*, which had Vivienne Leigh cast as the female lead. Because he has such a wealth of experience in the entertainment industry, the BBC would be well advised to allow him to conduct seminars for their aspiring young producers.

Ernest is also a charming gentleman who speaks very highly of Tommy. Being introduced to Ernest by Tommy a few years ago is certainly one of the highlights of my life, the fact that I have continued to enjoy his company from time to time and take pleasure in his conversation, is a rare privilege.

Of course like all the sixties boys Tommy would be called upon to go along to film studios at Pinewood to take part in some of the many British 'B' movies of the day. All passed without Tommy doing much more than walk around in the background, so he has no special memories of the films apart from being well paid for, them, as he put it, not acting just having a bit of fun.

One of the films that Tommy was invited to appear as a guest star in was called *Saturday Night Out* also starring The Searchers, this was a Comton-Cameo film also featuring people like the famous boxer from Tommy's younger days Freddie Mills. Having known Freddie, Tommy like many of us has never believed that the courageous battler who fought many times well above his weight, took his own life. It just would not have been in his nature to do so.

Tommy did star in one film though, his co-stars being that great actress Eleanor Summerfield and a man who was a household name for many British film goers, John Slater. The film was called *The Man with the Yellow Hat*, and the script involved Tommy as the leader of a motorcycle gang charging all over London chased by the police.

The outfit that Tommy wore was, to say the least, very bizarre; jeans with a studded leather codpiece, leather jacket and a yellow woolly hat. Under that hat was concealed a stolen painting and the escapades that Tommy had during the film trying to evade discovery and capture were for him very exciting. This is a story that certainly captures my imagination, I would hope to see this film at some point, as would members of Tommy's family. A young Derek Nimmo was also involved in the film and I have no doubt his presence added greatly to the proceedings.

If it was ever released, Tommy never saw it and because of that thinks it was probably not very good. A pity because he had hoped it would have given him the chance to get into serious acting, which he was, and even now is, still very keen to try. This is something I think will help to extend his career in the future.

I did try to get him a copy of the film for his sixty-fifth birthday but the British Film Institute quoted a price involving telephone numbers for a copy. Strange how people who hold archive material that may never see the light of day because it is perceived of having no value or relevant merit, always price the personal interest of people involved at far too high a level, so depriving people like Tommy's grandson, Bailey of the chance to see some of the things that his granddad achieved.

Tommy's recording career under the auspices of Norrie Paramour followed similar lines to 'Stars and Garters', *'Babbette'*, *'Let's Do It'*, and one of his most popular recordings *'Buttons and Bows'* are examples of the material that Tommy was doing, standards rather than just Rock and Roll.

It would seem Norrie had an inkling of the possibility of longevity in Tommy's career when he chose some of the old standards for him to record. Possibly realising that apart from the pleasure it would bring older record buyers to hear favourites from their youth, younger people would be attracted by the new arrangements and of course Tommy's unique voice.

It should be recognised at this point that Tommy's records all sold between seventy thousand and one hundred thousand copies with ease, many of them selling more. So while admittedly *'Ain't Misbehavin''* was by far and away the most successful and biggest hit, Tommy was not a one hit wonder, a fact recognised by Brian Matthew recently when he introduced three in a row of Tommy's hits during his great Saturday morning show on Radio Two, 'Sounds of the Sixties'.

As Norrie Paramour was the first to admit, he didn't always get it right. One example of this was making *'Sixteen Years Ago Tonight'* the B-side of *'Lavender Blue'*. As everyone realised afterwards, although *'Lavender Blue'* went on to be one of Tommy's signature songs, *'Sixteen Years Ago Tonight'* had the potential to be even bigger than *'Ain't Misbehavin''*.

When Tommy recorded *'Crazy About My Baby'* Norrie was really worried, saying 'Tommy you've really gone and done it now, you can sing. I don't know what to do, if I release this record you will either be the biggest thing ever or you will lose your following. Although the record was eventually released there was no push behind it and people would not really hear it until I put it out on a CD thirty years later.

An interesting story at the time of the record's release, Tommy bought a brand new Vauxhall Cresta car and just like the song he was crazy about it. He got up every morning and polished it and rubbed it down every evening, he could not have given it more loving care if it had been his baby. One evening he was driving home and an old lady stepped into the road without looking. Tommy swerved and wrapped the car round the lamppost. Because of his universal popularity the old lady recognised him and after telling him she was sorry said she would buy his record to make up for making him crash. Tommy smiled ruefully and thanked her. He still doesn't think it was a fair swap but as he says she was a nice old dear so couldn't be mad at her.

Tommy's good friend Johnny Kidd wrote a song he would have liked Tommy to record but Norrie was not sure, he thought that Johnny should record the song himself. Sadly Johnny would later die in a car accident on 8th October 1966, as Tommy says given the kind of man Johnny was, the tragic circumstances of the accident would have made it impossible for him to go on. Tommy remembers him as a really wonderful guy and still misses him today.

Johnny liked Tommy and really wanted him to record 'Shakin' All Over', after some time and argument Norrie finally relented and let Tommy record the song on the EP *Knockout*. It was greeted by a very positive response by the fans. Who knows if it would have been a hit for Tommy if it had been released as a single. Tommy says, 'the song was Johnny's and I'm just pleased to have recorded it and performed it my way'.

Tommy still sings this song in his act to this very day, always preceding it with the words 'this is Mr Johnny Kidd's great song *'Shakin' All Over'*. Audiences go wild and I think along with Cliff's *'Move It'* it must be considered a Rock'n'Roll anthem

As Tommy says he will never forget this lovely man, it was a privilege to know him. He can still see Johnny now in his mind's eye striding out on stage with a patch over one eye waving a cutlass over his head and then hurling it down into the stage where it would remain quivering while he performed. Although Tommy remembers one night when this flamboyant entrance nearly had serious repercussions. Johnny came on stage as usual, hurled the cutlass into the stage but didn't know it was a metal floor, there were sparks as the cutlass hit the stage and ricocheted into the audience nearly decapitating a couple of fans.

There are many amusing stories to come from Tommy's time on the road. We often recall the night that Heinz who loved to perform Rock and Roll resplendent in drape suit and brothel creepers leapt from the top of an amp onto the lid of the piano, only to find on this occasion that the lid had not been closed. The place was in uproar, the rest of the band laughed but kept playing, the piano player cursed, Heinz carried on singing while trying to free his feet from the strings. He finally leapt out minus his shoes, and finished the set in fluorescent yellow socks. The audience were on their feet laughing, clapping and shouting for more. When he got into the wings Heinz was furious, 'I should get double money', he fumed they got me as a bloody comedian as well as a singer. Later having calmed down he laughed at the memory himself. Indeed he often used to reminisce about it with Tommy and I as we travelled together up and down the country.

Pianos played a big part in funny stories about Heinz, I remember Con Cluskey from the Bachelors telling me that Heinz was on tour with them once. They had all arrived at a theatre to be told by the manager that a lovely grand piano had been made available, polished and tuned as requested. The manager then asked who played the piano? Con replied 'I don't know', same reply from his brother Dec. Then Heinz said 'it's for me'.

'Oh,' said the manager, 'you play then?'

'Oh no,' said Heinz, 'I just like jumping on top of them.'

The manager was furious and needless to say that was one piano Heinz didn't jump on.

Con and Dec are two really nice guys who have recorded some fabulous songs like *'Charmaine'*, and *'Diane'*. They are still touring and we see them from time to time. It is always a pleasure to be with them.

Wee Willie Harris is another one who has given us a good laugh on a few occasions, Willie has been a friend for a long time and we often work with him. One amusing incident in particular stands out above the rest. We were doing a show in Liverpool, Mike Berry and Albie Wycherly were also appearing that night. The compère was local radio presenter Frankie Connor. Who as a performer made more appearances at the famous Cavern Club than any other. Frankie is also, apart from being well thought of by Tommy and I, a very nice guy who is really well respected in his chosen profession.

Willie was on stage and really had the place rocking when in his excitement he decided to take his shirt off whirling it round over his head and really going for it. Suddenly a lady in the audience whipped off her bra and threw it to him, 'shouting here you are love, you need this more than I do'. Everyone on stage and those of us in the wings collapsed in fits of laughter.

That said Willie is one of the acts that always gives one hundred percent value for money. He has great skill as an entertainer.

Willie is without doubt one of the hardest workers in the business. He is also one of Tommy's long-standing friends in the business, we always enjoy ourselves in his company.

Clem Cattinni provided me with one of the cleverest pieces of humour in this section. Surprisingly he achieved it at Jess Conrad's expense. We were all up in Welshpool for the town's winter festival organised by Freda Davies and show promoter and entrepreneur Alan Crowe. I was doing an interview with six of the acts in the council chamber, Clem, Jess, Craig Douglas, the gorgeous Billie Davis, Graham Fenton and John Leyton. John had just finished telling the audience about the time he had spent with Elvis Presley. Clem seized his opportunity; 'have you ever met Elvis?' He asked Jess, with an innocent smile on his face.

'No,' replied Jess, 'I haven't.'

'Well don't worry,' said Clem, 'I'm sure that like the rest of us you will see him soon.'

The audience exploded with laughter as all of us on stage had ages ranging between sixty-one and seventy-two; there was no doubt what Clem was hinting at.

We cannot leave these humorous stories without telling a couple at Tommy's expense. Like the time with The Rapiers backing him on a show in Chingford, the promoter ran out to the front of the stage shouting 'lower'. Of course with the band playing Tommy couldn't hear him, so the guy resorted to putting his arms out from his side and lowering them. Tommy ever the wag realised what he meant but decided to have a laugh. The more the guy lowered his arms the lower Tommy crouched until he finished the song lying on the stage with the band and the crowd in fits of laughter. In the excitement the guy, not realising the band had stopped playing, then shouted out into the mike that was now level with his face, 'I mean you are too bloody loud!' Causing us all to break out in even more laughter.

One of the other hilarious occasions with The Rapiers occurred at the Butlin's camp in Pwelheli. We were discussing Tommy's set in the dressing room and what keys he would sing each song in and I gave them a list. Brad the bass player looked at it and said, *'Lavender Blue*'s' not in that key I've got the record and I know what key it's in.'

Both Tommy and I disagreed with him, Tommy saying 'I should bloody know what key it is I've been singing it for thirty-five years' and we thought that was the end of it. Everybody went on stage and when it came to *'Lavender Blue'* the band took Brad's view and played it in the key he'd said. It wasn't much fun for Tommy but he manfully stuck to his task. Unlike many artistes who would have stopped and blamed the band, Tommy fought his way to the end of the song. The key was way to high for him and he sounded like Tiny Tim on helium. When they came off stage Brad, very droll, said, 'I might have got that wrong', everybody including Tommy just collapsed in fits of laughter.

The Rapiers led by Colin Pryce-Jones are one of the finest bands around very professional and all brilliant musicians. Incidentally Brad tall, lean and athletic was the guy who climbed in and out of ladies bedrooms in the famous Cadbury's Milk Tray television adverts.

On another occasion we had gone up to the Adelphi Hotel in Liverpool to attend a dinner put on by the Chairwoman of The Variety Cub of Great Britain, Lynn Staunton. Lynn is a stunningly attractive lady who causes heads to turn whenever she walks into a room, more than this she possesses great organisational skills and business acumen. Lynn runs her own Entertainment Company Power Promotions with great skill.

The dinner was to celebrate the inauguration of a Sunshine Coach in the name of Billy Fury. The top table guests included Billy's mum Jean Wycherly, his brother Albie, Tommy, Jess Conrad, Joe Brown, PJ Proby, Vince Eager and his daughter, Lynn Staunton and Billy Butler. Normally I sit with Tom at these functions but on this occasion I sat on The Variety Club Table. This would prove significant as the evening wore on.

Tommy was a bit under the weather and so not eating, in fact he had barely eaten all day. Seated next to Vince Eager he found his wine glass filled by Vince every time he emptied it. By the time they were called on to make a speech, Tommy, not much of a drinker normally, was a little inebriated. He rose to his feet and told the story of the time he drove Billy's car home for him, ending by saying that he loved the guy and missed him very much. The trouble was, because of the drink, his cockney accent became broader and it was difficult to pick out everything he said. When Joe Brown a fellow cockney stood up he began by saying how nice it was to be back in Liverpool, although speaking in different dialects could sometimes be a problem, but that it was usually possible to understand each other. He then went on to say that he hadn't understood a fucking word that Tommy Bruce had said, so the rest of them must have had no bleedin' chance. The place was in uproar with Tommy leading the laughter.

Of course Tommy and the boys have always taken the chance to have a laugh at my expense. Like the time I introduced Heinz on stage in his hometown of Eastleigh. There was only one door from the dressing room and it led out on stage and you had to come out and go back the same way so I introduced Heinz and headed for the door only to find that Dave and Tommy had locked it. Thinking on my feet I saw a tambourine on the floor beside the drum kit so I picked it up and pretended to play it, I have no rhythm and can't even clap in time. At the end of the song I turned and saw Dave and Tommy standing in the open door roaring with laughter, I quickly left the stage and when we were all in the dressing room we all just collapsed in a heap, as Dave said now you are really in the business.

Of course we were not laughing later when the club secretary came in with pound coins cupped in his hands and dropped them on the table. 'Sorry lads,' he said, 'bit of a cock up, that's all we've got.' A total of £90 between three artistes a band and a compère, that as we say is show business. Every single artiste in the business has stories to tell about the nights they didn't get paid.

That said I am always mindful that Tommy's reputation must be protected, I paid the band out of my own pocket, even though I knew that we might never see them again. Word goes round and we have built a reputation that is now well-known in the business, Tommy Bruce and Dave Lodge will look after and pay you no matter what happens.

One of the best of the many compilation albums Tommy has appeared on was The Saturday Club album. This album was unique by today's standards because instead of using pre-recorded tracks, as is the norm now, Norman Newell, the man responsible in no small way for Danny Williams' success in the charts, took all the regular performers from the show hosted by Brian Matthew into EMI studios to record the tracks especially for the album.

Apart from Tommy a line up of artistes that included, Gary Mills, Marion Ryan, mother of twins Paul and Barry Ryan who would later enjoy chart success themselves, Ricky Valance, Keith

Kelly, Johnny Angel, King Brothers and The John Barry Seven. The aforementioned Brian Matthew spoke an introduction for the disc. The show's producer Derek Grant collaborated with Norman Newell in producing the disc. Although recorded in EMI studios the LP was released by Parlaphone. Norman Newell had previously been responsible for three highly successful LPs using the artistes from the television shows 'Six Five Special', 'Oh Boy' and 'Drumbeat'.

Of course there will always be a downside to any success and one of the worst events in Tommy's career came when he was booked to appear at a club in Northern Ireland. When Tommy flew in, he was aware of the troubles in the area but had no way of knowing just how bad things had become. It would turn out to be just about the worst gig of Tommy's career.

A man called Jim Ryan met Tommy at the airport, a nice guy who I met in 1999. He told Tommy if they were stopped to keep his mouth shut. 'If you speak it will probably cost you your life.' As they drove along he was telling Tommy what had happened while he was in the air, Tommy didn't doubt him for a minute. Cars on fire, people throwing stones and shouting and screaming in the streets all around him, the place was in chaos. Jim said he was taking Tommy to his hotel and on no account to leave his room until he came to take him to the club. It was Sunday evening, 30th January 1972 and Tommy was shocked to find he had arrived in the middle of one of the worst actions of the decade. It would go down in history as Bloody Sunday. Of course he had no idea just how bad things were until later.

When Jim picked him up they went straight to the club and Tommy got ready. When the band started playing he bounded on stage in his usual enthusiastic manner, only to find the audience standing with their backs to him, they remained in silence like that for his whole set. They just didn't want an English entertainer on this day of all days. To make matters worse Tommy was ex British Army, information that featured in his publicity. Jim drove Tommy back to the airport and put him on the plane. To this day Tommy has never been booked to re-appear in Northern Ireland.

Another of Tommy's trips would not be the great success it should have been. An English agent who thought he would make a killing on the entertainment scene after he had emigrated to New Zealand decided to bring Tommy out to tour Australia and New Zealand. For Tommy this was a great experience as always he made friends with people from all walks of life. One of the outstanding moments for him was when he was given a traditional Maori welcome. He regards that as one of the most flattering things that have been done for him in his whole life, he really enjoyed his time over there.

Unfortunately although the agent provided lots of bookings, he and the venues had not realised that Tommy needed musicians to back him. So Tommy would often turn up only to find that there was neither PA nor band on the premises so he would be unable to perform. In the end although Tommy was always paid, it was decided by mutual agreement that he should return home. It was hoped that when the entertainment scene realised the requirements for acts, Tommy would be invited back, as yet that has not happened.

Anita Harris presents Tommy
with an award

Stars and Garters

Tommy, Kathy Kirby and Clinton Ford
The Waiter, The Porter and The Upstairs Maid

Tommy and
Johnny Kidd

I first met Tommy at the Queens Theatre, Blackpool where we were booked for a three-month summer season, Tommy's record *'Ain't Misbehaving'* had climbed into the UK Top Ten charts, Larry Parnes was the promoter of the show that included Joe Brown, Georgie Fame, Peter Wynn, and our backing group 'Nero and the Gladiators'. I remember the first rehearsal well, Tommy, in gruff voice sang *'Great Balls Of Fire'*, we were all sitting in the front row and gave him a standing ovation. Then came my turn and the same thing happened, from that day on Tommy and I seemed to click.

Whenever I was on the stage he would be at the side trying to make me laugh, and likewise when he was performing, I would be watching too, before any of us went on stage he would say 'Kill 'em Nelly', that was the nickname he gave me thereafter. During that three months we became really great mates we were inseparable, I remember one night we got locked out of the hotel so we went back and slept in the dressing room of the Queens Theatre.

Following that summer season Larry Parnes signed us both to appear in his new show to tour England, called 'The Rock and Trad Show', on the bill was Billy Fury, Joe Brown, Duffy Power, Georgie Fame, along with The Vernon Girls, plus The Lord Rockingham Band, we played every major town in England, Tom and I shared the same dressing room and stayed in the same hotels throughout the tour. We had become almost like brothers and did things like horse riding when we were not touring. Following the Rock and Trad Show, we both sadly went our own ways, but always managed to stay in touch with each other.

The last time I saw Tommy was at the 'Lakeside', Bob Potter's new club, he didn't know I was there, until after the show. I knew Bob Potter very well and walked into Tommy's dressing room and said 'kill 'em Tommy', and he replied, 'kill 'em Nelly' not long

fter I got married and emigrated to Australia. Some twenty-five
ears later I was contacted by Dave Lodge who was writing this
ook on Tommy's life and he gave me Tommy's phone number,
nd his first words were; 'how are you Nelly what's happening?'
Ve talked at great length about our times together, he summed it
p by saying, 'whatever happens in the future we had a great
ime didn't we Nelly?'

Nelson Keene

The opening of a Chinese Restaurant

Chapter Fourteen

The music scene was changing new bands where coming in, The Beatles and the Rolling Stones were stealing the march on everyone, but Tommy and his Bruisers were still on the bill. He well remembers appearing with the Rolling Stones at Victoria Hall, Stoke on Trent. He recalls being amazed at the length of their hair. It wasn't just the music that was changes it was the hairstyles and fashions as well.

Also with them on the bill that night was a powerful young singer called Lee Curtis who went on to carve out a great career for himself in Germany. Lee had a recording contract with Decca at one stage but was released due to political manoeuvres behind the scenes. Also Brian Epstien was keen to sign him before he had signed The Beatles but Lee was managed by his brother who thought it would be better if Lee stayed in the family circle. Who knows what might have happened for Lee if a different decision had been taken.

Another show that should have had The Stones on the bill was 'The Southern Sounds Show', with Brian Poole and the Tremeloes topping the bill at New Brighton Tower. The Stones failed to turn up as big things were happening in their careers at this time; things that would go on to make them one of the biggest and longest lasting touring bands of all time.

Incidentally Tommy would return to The New Brighton forty years later as part of Doug Darroch's Operation Big Beat with a cast containing more of the Parne's boys on one bill than had been seen for many years. The cast included Marty Wilde, Terry Dene, Dave Sampson, Danny Rivers and Brian Gregg. Lance Fortune who sadly had suffered his second stroke and couldn't perform, still joined us in the audience.

It was a great evening I even managed to get Barry Mason along who hadn't seen Tommy on stage since they parted company forty years before. Barry said Tommy was great and that he had felt the same sick feeling in his stomach that he had felt all those years before at that first live gig on the Mike and Bernie Winters Show. Tommy's comment to the audience, delivered with his usual dry humour was, 'New Brighton I was here forty years ago, they take a long time to book you back don't they?'

In spite of The Beatles taking over the charts as the sixties progressed, Tommy was still in great demand because of his ability as a live performer. The BBC on one of their live shows made him top of the bill over The Animals, although they were riding high in the charts with *'House of the Rising Sun'* at the time, simply because of Tommy's crowd appeal.

Another instance of this was when, much to Tommy's surprise and as he admitted later, no small embarrassment, he closed the show when appearing with Vera Lynn and Dick Haymes. Tommy had great admiration for both of them, particularly Vera Lynn, as like many of us he had grown up listening to the wonderful songs she recorded in the war years. It says a lot for Tommy's performance that the audience went home happy that evening.

Also because of his versatility Tommy was able to appear in shows like 'The Good Old Days' with his natural timing and phrasing of the old songs. His brilliant interpretation of *'Life Is Just a Bowl Of Cherries'* being just one example of this, allied once again to his natural Cockney good humour and charm, had him in great demand for this kind of show.

These live shows gave Tommy the chance to ad lib and show his versatility. On one occasion he was appearing in a show for the BBC. Tommy had spent all day rehearsing a song, backed by Jack Parnell and his orchestra, about 'a bloody red Indian' and to put it mildly Tommy couldn't stand it. Its actual title was *'Coligah Was A Wooden Indian'*, an old Hank Williams' number, but Tommy had never heard of it, didn't like it and as far he was concerned it was instantly forgettable. So during the performance after singing the first verse, Tommy suddenly shouted take it away Jack and leapt off stage into the audience, something he still does to this day. Proceeding to shake hands with everyone, greeting them with; 'all right darlin', havin' a good time,' or for the men 'Allo mate 'ows it goin'. They loved him, after keeping Jack playing for the best part of five minutes he jumped back on the stage drawing his hand across his neck from left to right, the universal sign to end it. The audience were on their feet clapping and cheering, they loved him. Incidentally Tommy never sang the song again.

At this time Albert and Mildred Burgess came into Tommy and Sheila's life. They were fans who adored Tommy for his singing and became friends and helpmates along the way. Tommy and Sheila still appreciate all the efforts they made on their behalf.

Moving into the seventies, Tommy's abilities as an all round entertainer would come to the fore, he seemed just as relaxed as a cabaret artiste as he had been as an out and out Rock and Roller.

Weeks spent at the famous Batley Variety Club in Yorkshire and the Talk Of the North in Manchester were always enjoyable as they gave Tommy a chance to spend time with his northern fans. He has always enjoyed tremendous support in the north of England as has been shown by the continued loyalty of these fans. Once again this demonstrates the universal popularity he enjoys, because it goes without saying how popular he is in the south.

Various musicians came and went as Tommy tried to put bands together so that he could keep the show on the road. Guys like

Mickey Willets who played drums still keep in touch from time to time. Others like Graham Fenton's brother Ken Rankin, who is an excellent bass player who enhances any band he is with, are rarely heard from but will not be forgotten.

Tommy was appearing in Blackpool when he met Roy Hastings who was compèring a show there. Roy suggested that he could look after business for Tommy and that proved to be the case. Roy's knowledge of the northern entertainment scene brought in a level of work higher than Tommy had experienced since the Stars & Garters days, he was out every week up and down the north of England sometimes working two or three clubs a night. Incidentally Roy went on to be a very successful agent who I believe presently represents some of the most successful tribute acts around. I have spoken to him on a few occasions and he has fond memories of Tommy.

Sheila, being a northern girl welcomed this move, as it offered the opportunity for them to be near her family, initially they moved into a semi-detached house but as things got better they found a dream home. It was just outside Warrington in a village called Culcheth. It had half an acre of garden with a stream at the bottom plus a shop included in the price at the front. Offering the opportunity for them to grow and sell vegetables to sustain their life if gigs became thin on the ground. A fine example of forward planning as this was to prove one of Tommy's busiest periods.

Although busy as he was, he always found time for a game of golf with friends like actor Johnny Briggs, who has gone on to become a stalwart of the Coronation Street cast.

Tom O'Connor, the great Liverpool comedian, remembers one of these occasions when Tommy was doubling or trebling up very well. He was working the Kraft Margarine Club and Tommy was due to close the show but being held up at his previous venues, was late getting there. By the time he did get there Tom was trying to get through his own act for the third time, such efforts on behalf of Tommy and other artistes were not unusual.

While we are talking of comedians, Tommy remembers meeting the hilariously funny Jimmy Cricket around this time. He recalls, apart from Jimmy being very talented, he is a charming man who is great company. Indeed we were with Jimmy at one of Neil Crosland's get together dinners for friends of Charlie Williams, only a couple of years ago.

Diana Dors had a club in Manchester at this time and she asked Tommy and Sheila to look after it. This seemed like a good idea at the time, Sheila could manage it while Tommy was out gigging, then he could lend a hand in the club at other times. Unfortunately Alan Lake Dor's husband failed to understand that the club needed money to run. He would make trips north to collect the takings and leave Tommy and Sheila without the funds to pay the staff or the brewery. In the end having had enough, Tommy closed the club put the keys in an envelope and sent them to Dor's. She came up to see them in the hope of changing their minds but it was over for them, Tommy just could not work under those conditions.

At this time he was working for one or two local agents/ promoters in conjunction with Roy Hastings, Joe Pullen being one and Tom Ivors of Crème Entertainment another. In Joe's case Tommy found it a pleasure to work for him and was given lots of engagements by him including appearing at the popular venue, The Talk of the North. I spoke to Joe recently at a party for Maxine Barry and I found him still to be a man you could respect. As Tommy says the less said about Tom Ivors the better. It all ended acrimoniously and if Tommy and I had a pound for every time we were told by people like that, we would never work again, Tommy could have retired years ago, and lived in great comfort.

Things did not work out as they'd planned, their idyllic life in Sheila's dream home was just too good to last They were too busy gigging and networking to spend enough time growing the vegetables. Plus there was an established shop already thriving in the village, the whole plan and their lifestyle became a bone of contention between them. These things were made more difficult when the work was not as plentiful. Sheila took work in a local pub to try to compensate for the shop not taking off but all to no avail. The more they tried in their own way to make things right the worse their problems became.

Of course Tommy continued to work at this time and one of the shows he did was 'Heroes and Villains'. This show was filmed at The Dominion Theatre and all the proceeds went to charity. It has, up to this point, been one of the best selling charity videos ever made, raising an incredible amount of money.

Tommy also did a TV show for charity. The show was in aid of MS and was organised by Stuart Henry who suffered from this debilitating condition. The show was called 'Do You Remember' and apart from Tommy, Del Shannon, Jess Conrad and Kathy Kirby were among the other entertainers appearing that night.

It's funny how little things change careers and Tommy might well have become a star of West End musicals had the fickle finger of fate not pointed in the wrong direction. It was around 1970 when Tommy auditioned for one of the most successful shows of its time and passed the audition, only to have this glittering prize pulled from his grasp. The show was *Charlie Girl* and Joe Brown was a real tour-de-force in it, but after enjoying great success Joe decided it was time to move on to other things. So he let Tommy know his part would be up for grabs and told the producer he thought Tom was made for the part.

Tommy turned up for the audition full of enthusiasm and literally acted out the songs as required using the whole stage, everybody who was there was most impressed. Tommy saw a little figure coming out of the gloom at the back of the theatre, walking through the seats towards the stage nodding her head. When she got to the front she smiled and said, 'yes, you will do very nicely'. Tommy was stunned, standing there looking up at him smiling was Dame Anna Neagle who of course took the female lead in the show. He remembers that she was a lovely lady and he would have been proud to share a stage with her.

He left the theatre in a euphoric state there had been handshakes all round he had got the job; life simply couldn't be better. How quickly it would all change and once again leave Tommy wishing that he had a manager who would take care of him like Barry Mason had in the early days.

Tommy was told the theatre would close for a couple of weeks to refurbish the set then he would be straight into rehearsals. Unfortunately a new financial backer, an American, took over the show. He decided it needed a new perspective and so had Gerry Marsden cast in the role, Tommy who had not yet signed a contract was dropped like a stone.

The show opened and Gerry's enthusiastic charm and talent were much in evidence. However it seemed that the theatre going public had taken Joe's cockney way of performing the role to their hearts and the show did not have the length of run it had enjoyed previously.

Sometime later Joe and Tommy met and Joe wanted to know

why Tommy didn't get it, as he thought he was, as they say, a shoe in. Tommy explained what had happened and Joe was stunned and walked away shaking his head. So ended what could have been a great career in the West End. If anybody was ever born to play there it was Tommy Bruce.

The show did enjoy a revival in the eighties with Joe performing in it with a new co-star the fabulous dancer Cyd Charrise. This story of how things can go wrong in show business, only goes to prove that old saying, 'If it ain't broke don't fix it'.

In a long and successful career in show business I have represented many of the United Kingdom's foremost stars. Artistes of the calibre of Anthony Newley, Bob Monkhouse, Frankie Vaughan, Max Bygraves, Danny Williams and of course Sir Norman Wisdom. Tommy Bruce is worthy of his place in their company.

I have presented these artistes in shows at the country's finest venues for example The Royal Albert Hall and the London Palladium. I have also provided shows for the Royal Family at Buckingham Palace and St James Palace. All the above artistes appeared on them and I could never forget Tommy Bruce's appearances on these shows.

Tommy is part of a breed of entertainer that just doesn't seem to be around anymore. He is multi-talented, vocally he is as much at home singing jazz, swing and old time ballads as he is with the rock and roll that made his name. He is a great natural comedian and a wonderful dancer.

I have been involved in acting productions and have found that Tommy's talent extends in this direction as well. He is a fine actor and as he gets older I can see a long career playing character parts. When it comes to voice over work he has a distinctive voice, which will see him working in that field for many years to come.

You may think all round entertainer describes a jack of all trades, master of none. Not so in Tommy Bruce's case, no matter what he does he is never less than brilliant. The reason for that is that he always puts a hundred and ten percent into whatever he attempts. That, allied to his amazing talent, makes sure of his continued success.

This book is an excellent read I recommend it wholeheartedly. Dave Lodge the author and Tommy's manager has put a lot of time and effort into getting it right and the affection he has for Tommy is very clear. I do not think this book could have been written by anyone else.

Johnny Mans
Theatrical Impresario

I have such fond memories of working with Tommy on both *Stars and Garters* and other television shows. A handsome gentleman with of course that unique voice! If ever one of Tommy's records is played on the radio, listeners know immediately who is singing, any introduction quite superfluous

The last time we worked together was on an all star charity gala in London in the early eighties. Tommy was as kind as he had always been to me: acting as an unofficial doorman and minder outside my dressing room door so I wasn't disturbed while I prepared for my performance. I am delighted to pay tribute to this lovely man.

Kathy Kirby

Chapter Fifteen

It was during this period that I started to come into Tommy's life, if only in a small way at the beginning. I had always been a fan, buying his records as a teenager, I actually saw him with the Larry Parnes 'Rock and Trad' show when it came to Ardwick in Manchester, in fact my mother enjoyed listening to him and we often watched 'Stars & Garters' together in the early sixties when my father worked late.

Tommy was one of the few singers that I didn't hear the bellowed instruction from my father to 'turn that rubbish down', when I played my records on the family's shared Dansette record player. Great days, eight records ready to go each dropping one at a time onto the turntable. Well that was the theory anyway; quite often they all dropped at once causing great frustration especially after I had taken the trouble to stack them in order of preference.

My parent's opinion of Tommy showed then what is still true today that Tommy's charm appeals to young and old. Although my parents were younger then than I am now, so they probably didn't appreciate the old tag, I know I don't. Anyway to go back to Tommy's story, at this time he was living and performing in the north, my wife Margaret and I started to see more of him as a performer. We would often speak because he is so approachable, just a few words; 'hello, how are you? Great show, goodnight,' that sort of thing, nothing that would be particularly memorable for Tommy but very pleasant for us.

Then when Tommy moved back down south it seemed that we would loose touch, but after a few months he came to appear at the Fagin's Nightclub in Manchester so we went to see him. After the show we chatted and then walked out to our cars together. It was at this point that Tommy realised that he had locked his keys in the car and had to phone for the AA in order to get into it. Rather than leave him alone on the car park, (everyone else had gone), we decided to wait with him. Sometime passed by and as Tommy had a long journey in front of him I suggested he took my car and we would wait for the AA. He was surprised by my offer but realised it was the practical thing to do. We gave him our phone number so that we could arrange to meet up the next day and swap back. However just as he was about to leave, the AA arrived and got him into the car, he thanked us; we said our goodbyes and went our separate ways. Little did we know that, from what had just been, from our point of view, a one-sided interest in him, a friendship that would certainly change our lives had begun.

A few weeks later, while I was in the shower, Margaret

answered the phone to be asked if Dave was there, she said I was and asked who was calling, 'Tommy' came the reply, 'Tommy who?' Asked Margaret, 'Tommy Bruce', came the response. Margaret came to me in great excitement and not a little confusion wanting to know why he was phoning. I picked up the phone and Tom said, 'I'm lost, do you know how to get to where I'm appearing tonight?

I said I did. I then asked where he was so that I could direct him. He laughed and said he was sitting on a stool in a bar, he just wanted to know if Margaret and I would like to travel with him to the show.

This, although we did not know it then, would be the beginning of not just a friendship but a bond that would stand the test of time, not just on a personal level, but on a business front as well.

Tommy was undergoing great changes in his life at this time, things had not been going well on the home front, Sheila and he were struggling with their relationship and as the work had been getting thin on the ground they took the decision to sell up in Warrington and move back down south. It was the final blow to their marriage and although they tried to put things right, following the move their life together had run its course. Tom moved out and they began their separate lives, although to this day, the shared love and the wellbeing of their children is a bond that has never failed. Also during this time their good friend Albert died, as Tommy has said this period was one of the lowest in his life.

As the seventies ended a period that would last almost fifteen years started, a wonderful era of nostalgia for old teddy boys and girls like my wife Margaret and myself. It was the era of sixties festivals at the Butlins Holiday Camps, Barry Island was the first place we went to. Tommy, Heinz, Wee Willie Harris, Mike Berry, Jess Conrad and a host of other stars of the sixties would stay on the camp and entertain and mix with the fans. The fans for their part would be dressed in fifties and sixties gear. Great days with the girls twirling round the dance floor in their dirndl skirts and the guys sporting drape jackets and making a good effort at restoring their quiffs and DA's (more of that later).

At that time a lot of the boys including Tommy were backed at Butlins by a great band called, The Rapiers. These guys are stars in their own right and are still a highly successful band today, as they should be, led by the redoubtable Colin Pryce-Jones on lead guitar. He of course learned much of his trade when working as a bass player backing another great friend of Tommy's Frankie Vaughan.

Tommy was very sad when Frankie died in a car crash, as he says so many of the friends that he has made in show business were destined to die young, very often in tragic accidents.

Incidentally Tommy and the rest of the boys were delighted to see Mike Berry enjoy chart success at a later stage in his career with the lovely ballad, *'The Sunshine Of Your Smile'*. As Tommy said, 'if one of us can do it, who is to say it can't happen again'. Tommy would benefit from the generosity of Mike and his management team at this time when he was given the job of compèring the shows on Mike's subsequent tour.

One of those stars who must be mentioned is Tommy's good friend Graham Fenton. Graham worked really hard throughout the sixties in bands like The Houseshakers without gaining the recognition he deserved. Nobody was more pleased for him than Tommy when he finally achieved that elusive success in the Seventies with his great band Matchbox. Graham is a smashing bloke who has proved his friendship to Tommy and I many times over the years. We take great pleasure in his company whenever we meet up.

The guys in their drapes and crepes, the girls in their dirndl skirts and waspie belts. For some of us guys the DA and the quiff in our hair were not what they had been twenty years or so before, but the enthusiasm was there and we jived and bopped the nights away as we thrilled to sounds of our youth.

Mike Lee Taylor and Barry Collings realised the potential of these weekends and promoted them with great skill and enthusiasm at one point moving them down to Butlins at Bognor Regis where they remained for the duration of the shows. However Tommy's participation in these events came to an end in a way that still leaves a bad taste in the mouth.

The booking system changed hands and Tommy at first continued to be part of the events and I had taken several advance bookings for him. We received notification from the hospital that Tommy, who had suffered with ulcers for some years, had to go in to have them attended to.

I contacted the new agents providing medical certificates to explain the situation and was assured that on his recovery Tommy would be rebooked. They never booked him again. Their attitude was made all the more of an unpleasant issue as, whilst in hospital, Tommy was diagnosed with stomach cancer, requiring major surgery.

A great Rock 'n' Roll Guitarist, Chris Black who had worked with many of the sixties artistes came up with an idea along with his partner Didi Melba for a Legends of the Sixties Tour. This brought Tommy, Heinz, Jess Conrad, Cliff Bennett, Don Lang and Screamin' Lord Sutch together plus a powerful girl singer in the Tina Turner mould Cissie Stone. Backed by Chris Black and his Black Cats it made for a very exciting show.

Touring the UK was not enough for Chris who always sees the bigger picture so with his usual enthusiasm he decided to organise a tour of Spain. The idea being the show would appear in bullrings, these venues being big enough to accommodate the crowds he was sure would be in attendance. Sadly we will never know if he was right as the people he booked the bullrings through did not realise the importance of a stage and PA system being in place.

Stranded in their hotel Tommy and the other guys waited while Chris tried to sort things out. Unfortunately money was running low and the hotel wanted paying, as the bill was growing daily. Tommy, Don Lang and Cliff Bennett decided to cut their losses and fly back to the UK. It was a nervous time at the airport wondering if they had left it too late, as there was a chance they would be arrested if the hotel decided each was responsible for their own bill. Cliff Bennett was very forceful on behalf of the other guys, only to be told that there were no seats on the planes for the UK. In desperation he took tickets for internal flights to Milan. The guys still remember being charged extortionate prices for coffee there. They only just got out in time as the hotel management, out of patience, decided to call in the police so Heinz and the other guys were carted off to the cells. Only getting home eventually when ex-pat Ronnie Knight, who knew some of the guys, came to an arrangement with the local police chief to get them out, then he got them home to the UK via Gibraltar. Of course the irrepressible Chris Black and his faithful guitar Brenda The Fender were undaunted by this set back and continue to blow our minds with great playing and fantastic ideas.

When Tommy and I linked up again back in Manchester, he confided in me that Don had told him on the way back that he had cancer. Treatment or surgery was not an option only pain relief, it would only be a matter of time, I, like Tom, was saddened to hear this.

This show was a brilliant concept and although it did not succeed as well as they'd hoped, it was the forerunner of many more successful tours. Such as the 'Solid Gold' and 'Solid Silver Sixties' shows that came together through the hard work and dedication of Hal Carter in association with Flying Music. The 'Legends of the Sixties' Tour would also be the catalyst that would bring Tommy and his second wife Ida together.

There was at that time an excellent venue for sixties performers in Openshaw on the outskirts of Manchester called The Napoleon, later the Jive Inn. Great entertainers like Big Jim White who presented his dynamic 'Tribute to Elvis' show and Ronnie Grundy with his band Sweet Chariot were providing the entertainment there. Sweet Chariot are an excellent band and have achieved success wherever they performed. I worked with Ronnie when we both had a day job and I can honestly say he has the most wonderful voice and his rendition of John Mile's great song *'Music'* is the best I have ever heard.

As well as a wealth of local talent, including Rockin' Ricky well known from his days with the Rock and Roll band The Velvet

Collars and also known for his European hit recording of 'Someone Someone' and another good friend at the time Herm, known as Mr Moonlight. The list of great shows was endless and they always played to a packed house. After the 'Legends of the Sixties' show had appeared there, Tommy became a frequent performer at the venue along with Heinz, Jess Conrad, Screamin' Lord Sutch, Wee Willie Harris and Dave Sampson.

Chris Black and the Black Cats initially provided the backing, doing some great shows, we certainly enjoyed some wild nights when Chris and his beloved guitar, Brenda the Fender were around. Martin Symonds affectionately known as The Animal gave him some help with this, indeed at one time the organisation seemed to fall on his shoulders.

After a time when it became clear that other projects were taking Chris's interest, the then proprietor of the venue, a Mr Kelly, put a local band called Wall Street in to back the artistes. The band was very enthusiastic about being part of these fabulous sixties shows and provided some exciting and entertaining backing for the acts.

There were some changes to the line-up during this time but Tommy and I became great friends with the boys and for a while they became Tommy's permanent band in the north doing several venues with him.

Names that are never to be forgotten include Keith Loftus,

better known to us as Rockin' Ron Bacardi, known as this for the copious amounts of the spirit he can consume and still remain standing. He played lead and sometimes rhythm guitar he was also the band's main vocalist. He was and still is a smashing bloke who has done us lots of favours; he is one of the best rhythm players around and no slouch on lead either.

Peter Colleton the wildman of the band on bass, he's crazy, a complete nutter on stage when he comes off he is one of the most intelligent and articulate men you will ever meet. Danny Thurston, known as the gentleman was on keyboards and piano playing, enhancing the sound with every note he is a lovely guy who I hear has not been too well of late so we wish him good health in the future.

Originally Johnny Hart was on drums, he knew how to keep the band tight, a great player. Johnny is a lovely man and a talented drummer who Tommy and I liked very much and we were very sorry when he decided to call it a day. I recently heard from Johnny again and he has been helpful, along with Ida's daughter, Angie amongst others, in putting on a benefit for Tommy while he has been ill. Paul, affectionately known by all of us as Stacey, was a flamboyant and stylish replacement when Johnny retired. He always drove the girls wild with his rugged good looks and charm. The Very Reverend Ian Derby, nicknamed Rinswind, joined us sometimes on lead guitar. He had a special way with him apart from being a fine guitarist, he is a very intelligent man and we like him very much.

We also had a really nice guy, Big Bill Drain on saxophone a man who could really blow up a storm. I well remember many nights when Bill was blowing fit to bust with Tommy exhorting him to greater efforts with the words, 'show 'em how you can play Bill'.

We must never, could never, forget Graham Marshall the roadie who doubled with vocal harmony. Graham worked very hard keeping the show on the road, he humped the gear, and drove the van. I often smile when I miss the turn off at a roundabout and say to Tommy this is the Wall Street way to get there, because Graham would often make two or three rounds of the roundabout before he made his choice with us in hot pursuit, even though we had seen the exit. We were in convoy so with Tommy uttering the immortal words; 'what's appenin' I would just keep hurtling round behind Graham.

We well remember the night that Johnny Hart, something of an explosives expert who worked at that sort of thing for Granada TV, decided a small pyrotechnic display started by an explosion would get things going with a bang. It did, it blew the ceiling out and covered everyone in plaster and dust and filled the room with smoke. The proprietors of the venue, Droylsden Cricket Club, were not impressed to put it mildly. The boys were always game for a laugh but that was an expensive one.

All in all a good team and great company to be with. Worthy of special mention is the group's resident groupie Big Ma. She loves the boys and does everything she can to help them, and let's not forget the girls, Debbie and Anne.

There were lots of laughs on the road with these lads particularly while we were touring 'The Way It Was Show' in the late eighties. Tommy Bruce and Heinz were the principle stars. We also had a girl singer, who I named the classy lady, as support on many occasions, one Pat Francis. This lady was much admired by audiences and fellow performers alike for her powerful voice and attractive personality. At some of the bigger venues we would bring in by request other sixties artistes like Jess Conrad, Dave Sampson, Wee Willie Harris and Screamin' Lord Sutch.

We were unfortunate at this time to come across a man called Tony Davidson who at first seemed a decent enough man, but would soon show us how wrong we were.

He approached me over the phone asking if Tommy would be interested in recording an album. It would be done at Mike Maxfield's Court Yard Studios in Stockport. The connection with Mike was a great inducement as quite apart from the fact that he is The Dakotas, formerly the backing band for Billy J Kramer, an outstanding lead guitarist, a musician of great skill, and he has an excellent reputation in the business. I had known him as a schoolboy when his parents owned and ran an off-licence in Heaton Moor, Stockport. He also, as I recall, played with a band called Pete Maclain and the Clan in those days. Pete is a rock and roller of great local renown who still performs in the Stockport area to this day.

So it was decided we would make this recording with Wall Street backing Tommy. Incidentally, because they were able to back other sixties artistes, it was decided after Heinz and Wee Willie contacted me they would also record for Tony Davidson.

After a particularly difficult time in discussions with Tony, I said to Tommy, 'I don't think you should sign this contract because I can't see anything in it for you.' We discussed it going back and forth over the same ground until in the end Tommy and I decided not to sign. At this point Tony used the band as a lever saying he would not pay them unless Tommy signed the contract. After much discussion and argument Tommy finally signed at 3 o'clock in the morning. The boys being paid had been the deciding factor, they did not deserve to have worked so hard for nothing. This is a policy I have tried to maintain ever since, if anyone plays for Tommy and does the job right I have even paid out of my own pocket, Tommy's reputation must never be damaged by charlatans. Had I had more experience I would not have let the recordings take place without some sign of the finances before hand, nor would I have allowed Tony to take the masters in the circumstances.

To this day neither Tommy, nor the other artistes, has ever received a penny from these recordings, although I know they turned up in places as far away as Australia and Japan. Legally it seems that he did nothing wrong, although it is a pity he made his living this way because I found Tony to be a very likeable man and I am sorry he felt he had to operate in the way that he did.

At the same time we were running 'The Way It Was Show' Tommy was also making appearances on 'The Six Five Special Tour' with the Vernon Girls, Craig Douglas and of course Don Lang. During the tour Don's previously mentioned cancer worsened and sadly he went into hospital and died. A lovely man who was a great friend of Tommy's and is still sorely missed by those who knew him.

Jess Conrad was doing lots of shows with Tommy at this time. Both Tommy and I think the world of Jess and his lovely wife Rene, who incidentally was the Camay girl in the TV advert. We all know that Jess is the best looking man in show business, because he has told us. As Tommy says, 'Jess slaps up to slap up'. But Rene incredibly, is even more beautiful now than she was in her modelling days, more than this she is warm hearted and generous, a truly lovely person.

When I was asked by my dear friend and Tommy's manager, Dave Lodge to contribute a few paragraphs about my long-standing friendship with Tom, It suddenly occurred to me just how long standing it really is.

It was in fact in 1960 when we first set eyes on one another. At that time we were both successful recording artistes and were regularly appearing on the numerous package tours out at that time.

My first impression of Tom was that he was a really down to earth guy and that suited me fine. I had already had my fill of the so-called wannabe pop stars of the day. So Tom's attitude and humour was very refreshing. We got on very well and I remember one night in particular, we had both sneaked out in between shows to get something to eat, this was somewhat difficult at times because of the fans who used to wait around outside.

However on this occasion we managed it. As we were walking past a shop doorway, a kid loitering in there came out with a smart arse remark. Tom stopped, looked at me, turned and walked back. He stopped in front of the kid looked him straight in the eye and said, 'If you open your mouth again I'll fuckin' eatcha.' You should have seen the kid's face, it was priceless. I knew at that moment we were gonna be good friends.

Since then I have worked with Tom many times over the years and I have to say that his performance has never waned, neither has his sense of humour. This humour was demonstrated perfectly when he invited a couple of women back stage to meet me in a club in Manchester where we were both working. The venue didn't have a changing room as such so they provided what can only be described as a kiosk with a curtain across.

Of course we could only use it one at a time. I was in there having just come off stage, with my back to the curtain I was aking off my trousers and as I bent down to remove them I felt a hand close round my testicles and squeeze really hard. Due to the shock and the pain I yelled out loudly, my cry was heard throughout the club. Falling backwards through the curtain I saw the two young girls with Tommy standing behind them in hysterical fits of laughter. I could do no more than laugh with him.

Let me say in conclusion that it is my great pleasure to know Tom as a friend and a great performer all these years. I know he has not been well lately, so I will just say get well soon you old sod, I love you brother.

Ricky Valance

Chapter Sixteen

Another new face was coming into Tommy's life at this time a lady who would change things around for him and go on to become his wife, her name was Ida Spiller. A keen Tommy Bruce fan, she came to one of the shows with her friend Joan and Joan's daughter Kate. Ida, like Tom, had been married before; she also had three grown-up children, Mark, Angie and Lee. Each one of them is a credit to her and it seems as though they have all become an extended family for Tom.

After the show Joan asked Tom if he would come and say hello to Ida, which he did. He was knocked out by her, she was and still is, an attractive, petite and vivacious lady with a warm personality.

At that time Ida was landlady of The Crumpsall public house so she invited Tom back for a bite of supper he readily accepted and a new relationship was begun. The aforementioned Rocking Ricky appeared at The Crumpsall and through his performances there, he became and remains a good friend of Tommy and Ida.

It wasn't too long before they became an item, seeing more and more of each other, romance was definitely in the air. During this time however, things were not going too well for Tommy, not the least of his problems being the theft of his car while staying with Ida. Before he had time to tell me himself, a phone call came through to where I was working at the time. Tommy's address book with his name on was still in the car and a gentleman, finding the car with all four doors and the boot open outside the gates of Queens Park in Crumpsall, Manchester decided he would try and get in touch. Unfortunately Tommy had put our phone numbers under Dave and Margaret with no last name. So when the person who found it didn't get an answer from the home number he tried the work number. As he did not have my last name the girl on the switchboard took a guess and put him through to a different Dave. The Dave in question, Dave Wilson, didn't really know what the guy was talking about so just took the details of the location out of courtesy and didn't take the name of the caller. After he put the phone down he suddenly remembered that I was involved with Tommy so he came and told me about the call.

I immediately phoned our lead guitarist at the time Keith Loftus, Rockin' Ron Bacardi, and asked him to get up there as quickly as possible. This he did but unfortunately by the time he got there the car had been stolen again. By the time it was found this time, it had been stripped of everything that could be removed, wheels, seats, battery ecetera.

Transport is obviously vital to an entertainer so imagine

Tommy's shock when the insurance company refused to pay up because they intimated he had taken the car north to have it stolen. While this situation was being resolved I undertook to do all the driving in my car.

Sometimes people like Mac Poole would lend Tommy a vehicle to save driving to London to pick him up for northern gigs. However Tommy and I enjoyed our time on the road together so much so that Tommy has allowed it to continue to the present day. This book has been the result of Tommy's reminiscences as we drove along.

Due to my travelling further afield I became more involved in obtaining gigs in the southern half of the country. In the end, due to other considerations, it was no longer viable for Wall Street to continue backing Tommy as some of the lads had day jobs and couldn't just take off in the middle of the week for a gig in Portsmouth or wherever, so a new band would have to be found.

This would mean renewing the acquaintance of Mac Poole, who I first came to know when he was with the Black Cats. A great drummer, Mac is a fantastic guy certainly one of my closest friends in the business who to this day helps us to keep a band of talented musicians on stage with Tommy. These musicians include the redoubtable Roger McQue on lead guitar, Roger is a wonderful musician who has played for some great performers including Shakin' Stevens PJ Proby and Freddie Starr, he is also our MD,

Pete Windle on bass, Steve Bird on keyboards, Steve Yarrington on guitar. Others who have helped make up the band are Alan Lovel who went on to join the Swinging Blue Jeans after Colin Manley died, incidentally Colin played in that great Liverpool based band The Remo 4 along with another good friend of ours, Harry Prytheric. Adrian Brown, Martin (Animal) Symonds, Dave St James and Dave Lane are among some other fantastic musicians who have played for Tommy.

Worthy of special mention is Pete Oakman; Pete as Tommy says seems to have been around from the very beginning, both playing and travelling with Tommy. Apart from being a great bass player who counts being in Joe Brown's backing band The Bruvvers among his achievements, Pete is also a fine songwriter who will always be remembered for writing Joe's hit '*A Picture of You*'. More importantly from Tommy's point of view is the fact that Pete has always been a good friend. In fact Pete told me of one incident while on the road with Tommy, Billy Fury and Nelson Keene. They were all travelling in the same car when they decided to stop at a greasy spoon for a cup of tea. Tommy through the door first went to the counter and said to the lady, 'Four teas darlin' and a Firkin.'

'A Firkin she replied what's a Firkin?'

'A Firkin big piece of that Firkin Cake,' said Tommy flashing his most roguish smile.

Everybody was in fits of laughter including the lady herself who realised that Tommy had drawn her into uttering some rather risqué language. Pete says he often laughs at that memory of Tommy because it reminds him of the humour that was always part of touring.

Mac Poole has at various times also provided a backing band for another well-known entertainer from the sixties, Ricky Valance. Ricky and Tommy often worked on the same shows together so there was no real conflict in this. Ricky of course is famous for his hit recording of *'Tell Laura I Love Her'* and his powerful singing voice allied to the great ballads he performs, made a great contrast to Tommy's hard driving Rock'n'Roll songs when they appeared together.

It was around this time that Tommy would see Nelson Keene for the last time. Tommy was appearing at Bob Potters new club 'The Lakeside' and Nelly walked into the dressing room and said the immortal words, 'Kill 'em Tommy', to which he smiled and turned round saying 'Kill 'em Nelly.' They had a good talk after the show and Nelly told Tommy he was getting married and emigrating to Australia, Tommy wished him well but was sad to see him go. It would be twenty-five years until they spoke again.

I am pleased to be asked to provide my memories of Tommy Bruce for his biography. I toured with Tommy the first time I came to England in the sixties and found him to be a stand up kind of a guy. He was as I recall always cheerful and made the backstage area a happy place to be. That is important to all artistes as a lot of time is spent there.

As a performer I remember him as being very lively and like me he enjoys audience participation, often having the house lights up so he can talk to the crowd. Tommy knows that Rock and Roll is about people having a good time together.

I hear from Dave Lodge, the author of the book and also Tommy's friend and manager, that after being ill for sometime, Tommy has had good news from his doctor. So I am sure we are all looking forward to hearing that Tommy is back on stage doing what he does best Rockin' 'n' Rollin'.

Freddy Boom Boom Cannon
Hit recording artiste and film actor

Chapter Seventeen

This was probably one of our most successful periods work-wise. Although I was finding out the hard way that phrases like 'the cheque is in the post' really meant you're not getting paid. Tommy had taken a gig down in Burnham-on-Sea and as I was now doing the driving I drove down from Oldham to Watford to pick him up. When I arrived I found Tommy somewhat concerned by his overdue poll tax payment. In fact he said we would have to cancel all his gigs, as he fully expected to get locked up as he had been summoned to appear in court the next week. I couldn't believe he had been worrying so much and had not told me about his problem. It was Friday and there would be no chance of avoiding going to court if it wasn't paid before Monday. As we were travelling back up north after the show Tommy would not be able to pay on Monday but would not have the money till he was paid his £150.00 fee.

'No problem,' I said. 'I have enough, we'll go to the Town Hall now and pay it, you can reimburse me after the show.'

This left us a bit short of travelling money but I had filled up with petrol before getting to Tom's so we would be okay. We stopped at a service station just before we got there to top up the petrol and get Tommy the usual pint of milk and some cigarettes and that was the end of our money. When we arrived at the venue, The Night Owl Caravan Park, we met up with the other artistes who were appearing there and decided that as the band needed to set up and Tommy wouldn't be on stage for some hours we would go to the café. This could have been a problem but I routed around in the glove compartment of the car and managed, with a bit of change that Tommy and I had in our pockets, to raise the price of a tea, a coffee and two buttered scones, everybody else was tucking into a full meal. Billie Davis who was on the bill that night turned and said 'what's the matter boys not hungry?' Although we were absolutely starving we both replied, 'no, we will have something later'.

Billie is one of the loveliest and hardest working people in show business. She always thinks of others and it is a complete delight to know her and spend time in her company.

We were then fortunate enough to sell two cassettes to a couple of fans. So we had a little money and Tommy decided to buy another packet of fags. By the time the show was over we were starving and thinking of good things like pie and mash to eat. So Tommy went to Mark Lundquist who, apart from being the lead guitarist on the night, was also representing the John Mill's office. 'Have you got the bread (money)?' Tommy asked.

'It's a cheque Tommy,' Mark replied.

Our hearts sank, we looked at each other, then Tommy said, 'it was supposed to be cash Mark.'

'Oh it got changed Tommy,' he replied.

We were stunned, after a pause Tommy said, 'okay give us the kite (cheque) then.'

'Sorry Tom it's being paid in fourteen days.' replied Mark.

So began one of our worst ever journeys home. With a trip of over four hundred miles ahead of us we made the decision to spend the £8.00 that we had left from the sale of the cassettes on petrol and try and get home to my house in Oldham. We wouldn't stop off at Tommy's for something to eat as that would mean going out of our way and using petrol we didn't have. It was a good effort and we nearly made it finally running out of petrol about thirty miles from home at six o'clock in the morning on the Yorkshire side of the Woodhead Pass. Leaving Tommy in the car, I walked about a mile to the nearest phone box and called my friend, Peter Leonard, and asked him to bring us a can of petrol. As I walked ruefully back to the car I thought that Tommy would think I was a waste of space and would definitely replace me with someone who knew what he was doing.

I arrived back to find Tommy and the car surrounded by a flock of sheep, he said they were the best audience he'd had in a long time. We often pass the same place on our journeys home and it always makes us smile. I learned some valuable lessons on that trip, never travel without a credit card and mobile phone and if I must be paid by cheque, get it a week in advance. A couple of weeks later Tommy told me that far from him wanting to ditch me, he thought that I would probably not want to continue with him. That is one of the things that helped cement our friendship.

For a while it seemed that nothing would go right we would have one good gig and the next would be a disaster. We did a gig at Heywood Civic Centre one week, which went well apart from my dry sense of humour not being appreciated by the promoter, John Sweetmore. Another lesson learnt, keep my mouth shut on subjects I know too little about.

Incidentally doing the backing for the solo acts who appeared that night including Tommy, Ricky Valance and the Vernon girls were a great bunch of lads The Colin Irving Trio. If only I could have retained their services for the following week I could have save a lot of problems and heartache.

The Swinging Blue Jeans closed the show, with their normal fantastic set. The leader of the group Ray Ennis is a great guy and Tommy has lots of good memories of him over the years. Both Colin Manley who was an unbelievable guitarist was with the band and Les Braid on bass a cracking bloke with a dry sense of humour would both die from cancer in the future. They are greatly missed.

Speaking of Les's sense of humour reminds me of Ray speaking at his funeral. Ray told us that he had gone to see Les near the end and said to him, 'It's all right for you, I am worn out on this tour, while you lie here resting.'

'All right,' replied Les, how do you think I feel? My career ended in Skegness, Why couldn't it have been the Albert Hall?'

I may not have remembered it exactly as Ray told it but I do think it is a fitting epitaph to a good and brave man, who is sorely missed by everyone who knew him. The following week I had taken a booking from Ray Martin, for Tommy to appear at the Robin Hood Caravan Park in Skegness and as I was singing at the time with me as support. Ray is a talented and flamboyant drummer who at that time was backing Brian Poole with his excellent band Electrix. Ray had his own agency and had given Tommy gigs previously, including a tour of Germany with Brian Poole so it seemed that all would go well, how wrong I was. With the benefit of hindsight I wouldn't have taken the gig as the writing was on the wall from the outset.

At the time Tommy was between bands, so I made the mistake of thinking I could put one in for him. Unfortunately the money was not sufficient to get all the musicians I would normally have asked. I asked a guy we knew Dave Dix who played saxophone with our good mate Screamin' Lord Sutch's band if he would put a line up together for the show. This he did but a couple of days prior to the show he phoned to say they had picked up a couple of gigs in France for very good money so they wouldn't be able to play for Tommy. Then I made my second mistake, I decided to save the gig by phoning the Musicians Union for a band to back Tommy. They were very helpful and put me in touch with a trio, who were very pleasant and took the gig. We all arrived at the venue for an afternoon band call and sound check. Then I made my next mistake. The camp had a summer show and it was plain we were surplus to requirements, as we could not get the sound check. We needed one as we were using the house PA but the soundman would not make himself available to us. After a discussion with Tommy we decided to manage without one, we were sure the sound would be fine as we would not be on till midnight and the show would have been going on for sometime then. We couldn't have a band call to rehearse the numbers but the guys could read so there should be no problem.

Another mistake, Tommy and I started to get worried when the drummer started to say he didn't think they could do the job. The keyboard player and the guitarist said it was just nerves and he would be all right when we got on stage. I wish we had listened to him, as he was the only one of the three who had the courage to speak up, instead of keeping quiet and hoping for the best. When it was finally time to go onstage I went out and began my performance, I never blame the musicians when things don't go well, but as Tommy said to our wives listening in the dressing room, 'they are killing him out there.'

The band simply were not playing what I was singing and the abuse from the crowd was frightening. It came to a head when I was singing Al Hibbler's arrangement of *'Unchained Melody'* at this point the musical director of the resident show told me he sank to his knees in disbelief, the band played three different tunes before I opened my mouth. None of which bore much resemblance to the song I was singing.

It was a good-sized audience and it sounded as if they were all telling me to get off, or words to that effect. I looked at the keyboard player to tell him to cut it at the middle eight but he was in a world of his own not looking at me, in fact totally unaware of me.

At the end of the song the place was in uproar I actually feared violence, but I couldn't come off because Tommy would have had to do longer so I just kept going. By the end of my set I seemed to have got the sympathy vote and left the stage with about half the audience on my side. It was at this point the MD said he thought that my performance had been one of the bravest things that he had ever seen. He added that he had known people run from the stage for less.

Worse was to come Tommy took the stage and whether the band had completely lost their nerve I don't know, they simply couldn't play for him. After the lead guitarist had failed to play the solo's in *'Shakin' All Over'* and *'Johnny Be Good'* Tommy's set was cut short.

When the band came off stage they said they couldn't understand the audience's attitude as they thought it had gone quite well. I was speechless.

With justified trepidation I went to pick up the money. As I walked through the crowd unrecognised from my time on stage, I was pleased to hear comments to the effect that people had seen our show in Birmingham before coming on holiday and that Tommy Bruce was absolutely brilliant and that I had been okay. They couldn't understand what had gone wrong. I got to the office to find they were refusing to pay, after some discussion I managed to get Tommy's fee but there was no way they would pay the band. I went back and told them the situation, they took it quite well at that point but a couple days later I got a phone call saying that if I didn't pay they would have to sue me.

I put the phone down and phoned the Musician's Union, telling them the whole story and saying that Tommy and I doubted the bands ability to read music. I was told I would not hear anymore from the band and I didn't. It's a pity because they were three nice guys who I am sure performed well in their own environment.

That wasn't all when we came out of the theatre we found we had two flat tyres, one I was able blow up with the foot pump, the other I had to change the wheel. We dealt with some very unpleasant people who didn't want to pay but I learnt a lesson, I haven't made those mistakes since.

An interesting footnote to this gig a few weeks later The Robin Hood Caravan Park was robbed and their whole summer's takings went from the safe. Rumours abounded that Tommy Bruce and Dave Lodge had taken their revenge, foolishness, but I will say it couldn't have happened to nicer people.

Some time later I had occasion to find myself on the wrong side of the previously mentioned Don Arden the Godfather of Rock and Roll. This really livened me up. Don had come up the hard way as a vocal entertainer of considerable talent and with the advent of rock and roll he moved into management and promotion. He was the first man to bring over the American Stars like Gene Vincent, Little Richard, Jerry Lee Lewis and Eddie Cochrane. Later he managed bands like The Small Faces, The Move and famously Black Sabbath. Incidentally his daughter Sharon married Ozzie Osborne, she of course went on to be a television presenter and a judge on the X-factor programme.

Don didn't suffer fools gladly and when I suggested over the phone that Tommy might be owed something, he blasted me to hell and back saying that the business was full of know-nothing pricks like me and if I knew what was good for me I wouldn't be phoning again.

I relayed this information to Tommy who said, 'tell him not to worry about it, Charlie will sort it out for me, Don knows Charlie and I go back a long way.' Charlie being Charlie Kray. We went down to The Cricketers Pub at Whips Cross where Tommy knew Charlie would be, he had a few words with him and I believe Charlie made a call, then told Tommy it would be all right.

When I got back to the house I, not without some apprehension made the call to Don Arden. He had never taken a backward step in his life so I knew he wouldn't be afraid but I told him what had been said. I do not know whether Charlie had been in touch, but I suspect that he had.

Don must have thought I had a bit more about me than he had at first thought as I had called him back. Although he said he was not in the least intimidated by the thought that Charlie had been in touch we came to an amicable arrangement. I for my part just put the whole thing down to experience. I never had occasion to speak to him again but he taught me a valuable lesson that I had occasion to be glad of soon afterwards.

We had secured a gig at a venue in Bolton and things had gone well so much so that Tommy was booked back for a second and then third time. It was the third time that problems arose. The man who owned the place Ian Boseman was a nice guy and up to that point we had got on really well. He was and I am sure still is generous to a fault always providing everyone involved with the show a beautifully cooked meal as well as a generous fee. He phoned me up at midnight on the night prior to the gig and said that as he was double booked Tommy wouldn't be appearing. He was sorry but that Tommy would be on the next one. I said this was unacceptable as Tommy had already had the expense of travelling up from London. So began a series of phone calls that went on until the early hours of the morning. Finally he agreed to pay Tommy his full fee, he said I would have to go and collect it the next evening. At that time I had no idea what was in store for me.

Tommy and I drove over to Bolton, arriving at the club at about six-thirty. When we got there one of the doormen went to tell Ian Boseman that we had arrived, he came back and said I could go in but Tommy Bruce was to be kept outside. I went in and was immediately surrounded by about half a dozen heavies. Not quite the welcome I had expected, to say I felt apprehensive was an understatement. The next thing Ian presented me with was a demand for a receipt on company headed notepaper. I was totally unprepared; this coming from a man who had always dealt in cash and provided his own receipts was something of a surprise. He gave me one of the venues own paper table napkins and with hands shaking I wrote him a receipt. Then I received a tirade of abuse and threats from him about what he thought of me, what I was doing and what he could have done to me. With his heavies closing in I was in no doubt that I was in trouble.

I remembered Don Arden at this time and instead of retreating I stepped forward and just said, 'I'm not worried about these guys, my priority is you paying Tommy's money'. I don't know if I dropped it through nerves, or he threw it at me, possibly he threw it at me, as he was not quite sure how to take my response.

I picked up the money and I thought I had better count it for effect. He then said, 'you have lost a friend and you and Tommy Bruce will never work again' I left with his abuse still ringing in my ears. I was sorry he felt like that but I had to get Tommy paid. Ian is a smashing guy and I really wish we hadn't had to fall out.

Looking back I think the heavies were not really meant as a threat, so much, as to make sure that I didn't get out of line with Ian in my efforts to get Tommy paid. In any event I bear Ian no malice and thank him for the good times we did have.

When I got back to Tommy and told him he said, 'now you see how it works, this will go round and people in the business will say Tommy's manager always gets the money.' It was a long time before anyone tried not paying again. I had fronted up on Tommy's behalf but I was still shaking when we got home.

I was at this point promoting and touring 'The Way It Was' show with Tommy Bruce and Heinz. This show was the most successful we had had so far. We toured the working men's clubs sometimes bringing in Jess Conrad, Dave Sampson and Wee Willie Harris. We were also using a very talented girl singer Pat Francis.

Pat as I have mentioned before was and is quite stunning with a great personality and a powerful voice. She always enhanced any show we put her in.

During this time Chris Black introduced Tommy and I to Graham Bodman. Graham seemed to be what we had been looking for; a successful promoter a man with, so it seemed, the business acumen to take Tommy back to the top of the tree. Initially it seemed that all would go well theatre dates came in and Tommy was working with other names of the sixties and fifties Ruby Murray, Danny Williams and Ricky Valance to name but three.

Tommy appeared on Graham Cole's Telstar Tour with Billie Davis, John Leyton, Cliff Bennett and the Rebel Rousers, The Honeycombes and of course Clem Cattinni's Tornados. Clem is one of nature's gentlemen and remains a close friend to Tommy and I to this day. Often stepping in to play for Tommy when our regular drummer Mac Poole is not available.

Graham Bodman planned a huge tour featuring all the names from the sixties and it really seemed that Tommy was on his way at last. Peter Lee Sterling who had been with Tommy in The Bruisers worked with him again and time was spent in Bill Farley's Blue Bell Recording Studio.

Bill was a great guy who had been a record plugger in the sixties. He was also a record producer who had worked on the Rolling Stones hit *'I see A Red Door and I want to Paint It*

Black'. Sadly Bill died in 2004 we miss him very much. In spite of continued financial reversals, which would have broken lesser men, he continued to remain cheerful and as the saying goes travelled hopefully.

We did quite a few gigs with Ricky Valance at this time and so spent time with Ricky and his wife Evelyn, affectionately known as Ev. Ricky is a perfectionist who likes things to be right and a few people criticise him for this. I can only say that Tommy and I have always enjoyed his company and no-one can deny he has a great voice. Ev is a lovely lady who always makes any dressing room feel like home.

Ricky should have had more hits, songs like *'Don't Play Number Nine On The Juke Box'* should have ensured more time in the charts but the vagaries of record company promotion and behind the scenes political problems prevented this. In spite of this Ricky still has a thriving live act that the public always turn out to see.

Another guy we have come into contact with along the way is John Alison. He was one half of The Alisons a vocal duo who enjoyed great success in the sixties both in the charts and on the Eurovision song contest with the self penned song *'Are You Sure'*. The other member of the duo Bob retired from the business, so John at various times tried working with different partners with varying degrees of success. In fact one of the times they appeared with Tommy was on the Jerry Lee Lewis Show. At the present time John continues to perform as a self-contained act.

Things were buzzing although we did have the odd setback, on one occasion Graham booked Tommy in at Butlins in Ayr, Scotland and apart from the journey we had a very strange reception. We arrived and it was plain that we were not welcome but things would get worse when we gave the resident band Tommy's set list they started telling us the songs he couldn't do because someone else on the show already did them.

The songs he was not to perform were his opening number *'Chantilly Lace'* a couple of others and unbelievably *'Ain't Misbehavin'* a long argument ensued and in the end Tommy sang them all but there was an atmosphere all night, we were very glad to hit the road home. In spite of this small setback, Tommy and I were very optimistic about the future.

It was even thought by Graham and I that a stage show working to the format of 'Stars and Garters' would be a good idea. It had been done before with some success as a summer show several years previously. So with this in mind we set about contacting the performers from the original show. This actually brought me into contact with James Harman an actor and playwright who represents Kathy Kirby. James has since become a friend, unfortunately he told me that Kathy was no longer able to perform.

We did manage to contact Clinton Ford, Vince Hill and Ray

Martine all of whom were interested in taking part in this venture. Incidentally Ray Martine stayed in contact with us and remained our friend until his untimely death. The stumbling block was Kathy, how could we possibly do the show without her?

At this point I suggested Kim Cordell, as she had been in the show and had, we felt, the right kind of personality added to a powerful voice that would help things go with a bang. Graham agreed, as did Tommy so I continued my search. I was fortunate enough to find her but having had an operation on her throat she was no longer able to sing. We shelved our plans after that and the show was never to be. The good thing to come out of this is that Kim and her husband Peter have remained in contact as our friends to this day, we often chat and have a laugh about the old days.

Of course there were still opportunities for me to cock things up on Tommy's behalf and the one I am writing about here has to be a classic of massive proportions. It was more by luck than good judgement I wasn't locked up, leaving Tommy to find a new manager.

We had been doing a few shows with Danny Williams at that time, as Graham Bodman was his personal manager, so we were pleased to have another gig with Danny, the venue was the Metropolitan Police Club. In the light of what happened it is probably better that I don't reveal the exact location of the venue.

Also appearing that night was the incredibly talented vocal impressionist Paul Melba. The backing was provided by Paul Roberts with his talented group Flying High as was often the case. I was as usual compèring.

As things were going very well at that time Tommy had two gigs that night the other one being at The Edmonton Theatre, Silver Street in Edmonton. Appearing with him on that show was Susan Maughan and Jess Conrad the show compère was DJ David Hamilton. The reason for telling you this is that Tommy's second appearance had great bearing on what happened at the Metropolitan Police Club.

Paul Melba opened the show and as always gave an unbelievable performance. Tommy eager to be on his way across town came on and quite simply gave one of his most powerful performances. As Nelly would have said, 'he killed 'em.' I was standing in the wings with Danny and the place was in uproar. Tommy was on fire, the audience were on their feet for almost his whole act, I look back and still can't quite believe just how good he was that night. Of course that's how it is with Tommy he always borders between great and fantastic and that night he was fantastic.

Danny stood in the wings in total disbelief, 'how can I follow that?' he asked.

'Don't worry Danny,' I said, 'you will be great, Tommy is

Tommy but you are Danny Williams and the audience will love you, you are the best at what you do. Just keep that in mind and you will be fine.'

Tommy came off stage and I thought there was going to be a riot he came back for his encore and then, like Elvis, he really did leave the building. For Danny's sake I stayed out there talking and telling jokes for at least ten minutes. Then I introduced him and just like I knew he would, he came out and completely captivated the audience. He gave a perfect performance and finally left the stage to his own standing ovation.

The show was over, we had been given an office to get changed in, which I was doing when I noticed a phone covered in dust with the number in the middle of the dial. I then made one of the most stupid decisions in the history of the world, I copied down the number into my diary. My reasoning being the show had gone so well that if we were not booked back after twelve months I would phone up and try and get the gig myself.

A year later I made the call, little did I know the panic that would ensue. The number had been designated as a line that terrorists should ring to give advance warning of a bomb being placed. When someone answered I cheerfully said, 'Hi, my name's Dave Lodge and I am Tommy Bruce's manager, we had a great show at your venue last year. Tommy, Danny Williams and Paul Melba blew the place away so I wondered if you would like to re-book the show?'

There was a long silence then a voice said, 'what's your number?'

I gave it and he said, 'we will call you back,' and hung up.

A short time passed then my phone rang and a different voice said, 'this is Scotland Yard would you like to explain how you came to be in possession of this number?'

I nearly choked then I stammeringly gave my explanation about having seen the number when getting changed. I was then told that I had put everyone on full alert and if it wasn't so obvious that I was a complete idiot and the stupidest man alive I would have been arrested. Needless to say I never rang the number again. Strangely enough none of us ever got booked to appear at that venue again.

We still continued to thrive at this time until at the very height of all the planning Graham Bodman suffered some serious financial reverses. He had planned a massive sixties tour involving most, if not all, the sixties stars of the day who were still performing. He got me to invest as he thought I should have a bigger share of the profits because we worked well together. I did as he asked and because we had come to trust each other so well we just shook hands nothing in writing. This would be both a good and bad thing in the future. We had promoted the tour well and we had excellent advanced sales, things were looking good.

Then I received a phone call, he opened in the usual way, saying, 'hello BF,' in his gruff voice, BF was short for Best Friend and he always greeted me in this way. I told him I knew it was really short for Bastard Face, we used to have a good laugh over this. He asked me to come and see him as he said he had great news to share with me. I drove down to Worcester to see him and he told me the news.

Graham had spoken to Roy Wood and arranged to promote a tour for him. We would fund the tour from advance sale money we had taken for the sixties tour. It would start immediately, advertise itself and be self-promoting. I was sure he knew what he was doing and had no hesitation in supporting him. It was a disaster because there had been no advance publicity, ticket sales were low and by the third night at the De Montfort Hall Leicester, Graham had no alternative but to pull the rest of the tour.

This proved to be catastrophic because everybody involved wanted paying and Graham had no choice but to pay as much as he could. In order to do this he had to go much deeper into the money from the sixties tour than he anticipated, when people heard he was in trouble they descended like vultures and the wheels came off for all of us in a big way. I personally lost an incredible amount of money, in three figures and have never completely recovered it. The sixties tour had to be cancelled and we were facing financial ruin.

However, Graham was nothing if not a fighter and together we set about picking up the pieces. We had never had a contract; just a mutual trust so nothing was ever on paper but I was never in any doubt that Graham would meet his obligations to me. Just as things started to pick up for us again Graham became ill and died from pneumonia within a few days, leaving Tommy and I facing financial ruin on our own.

Luckily Graham had been a good teacher and I was a fast learner, so slowly but surely between us Tommy and I got the show back on the road. We have no ill feeling towards Graham, had it not been for his advice I could not have accomplished the things that have happened to keep Tommy working. Whatever other people may think of him, Tommy and I know we lost a really good friend when Graham died. I have never found anyone else in his position in the business with whom I could share the same trust.

Tommy and Heinz

With Kim Cordell

Tommy and Chris

Tommy and Billy O'Keefe

I have fond memories of Tommy Bruce dating back to 1966 when I would book Tommy and other of the sixties performers through George Cooper and Harry Dawson. They all would come to stay at my then home in Undercliffe, Bradford. Tommy and the other guys Gene Vincent, Nelson Keene, Vince Eager and Michael Cox would go horse riding together and have great fun. I remember one occasion as we rode around Apperley Bridge when Tommy's horse got the bit between his teeth and ran off with him, we were all helpless with laughter as he struggled to regain control while shouting out expletives in his gruff cockney accent.

On other occasions we would party together and other people like Ricky Valance and Mike Berry would join us. Tommy always had a good sense of humour and they were great times I enjoyed getting to know the boys personally and we have remained friends through the years.

I got to know Dave Lodge about thirty years ago through Tommy and we became friends as a result of that association. Dave has worked hard on Tommy's behalf and I am glad that he is the one who has written this book. I know he has written it with great affection for Tommy and tried very hard to make the people who have known Tommy through his life an important part of the story.

Garth Kaywood
Promoter and Agent

Chapter Eighteen

It was at this time I started to discuss the possibility of licensing some of Tommy's tracks out from EMI. I had previously asked them to release a CD themselves, but they replied there was no interest. There were some really good songs on Tommy's discography which people were not aware that he had recorded, either because there had been no push behind their release or they never even got considered for release at the time.

After first being quoted a fee of £2,000 for a license I reminded them of their own words, 'there is no market', saying, if that is the case you should be grateful I am willing to take a chance and give you anything. They reconsidered and charged me £500.00 for what they termed a non-specific license.

The CD was a great success it sold well on the gigs and earned us money and provided EMI with a few royalties. James Cullinan of Finbar International took several copies and gave us a great review in his magazine. People like James play a more important part in keeping sixties music going than they realise, they do more than just sell it, they create an awareness of it.

We also received tremendous support from Terry Jones

through his Spinning Disc record shop. He and his lovely wife Chris organised a signing day in the shop which was a great success. It was a wonderful sight to greet us when we arrived, fans queuing down Chiswick High Street. Chris provided refreshments and with her bubbly personality helped to make it a fantastic event, although it has to be said we almost didn't make it. I drove down from the north to pick Tommy up. I have made the same journey without any untoward events more times than I care to remember, but on this occasion when I was coming round the roundabout near Tommy's home I heard a tremendous crash behind me. I looked in the rear view mirror and saw that a motorcyclist had gone down and was trapped under his bike. It was a very busy day because it was Saturday and the local football team were playing at home therefore several cars were just clipping the bike and causing it to rock up and down on the rider. I pulled up as I came off the roundabout and whilst phoning for an ambulance on my mobile phone, ran back through the traffic towards the fallen rider. As a former motorcyclist myself I felt great sympathy for him. I should have known better, as no good deed goes unpunished. I could see he was in great pain so in spite of the risk of being hit by a car myself I lifted the bike off him and put it on the grassed central area of the roundabout.

I asked if he thought he could get up but he said he was in too much pain, so I stood astride him to protect him from the vehicles that continued to rush round him. I spent about fifteen minutes in this position until no less than six police cars and one ambulance arrived.

The police immediately asked him what had happened and he said he had clipped the back of my car with his handlebar and gone down. I replied that this was rubbish pointing to my car and saying, 'there is not a mark on it and if a bike of that size had hit it, there certainly would be.' One of the policemen said, 'right you two get your cars and block him in case he tries to make a run for it.'

I said, 'you have got to be joking, why would I make a run for it? I have been standing here for the best part of a quarter of an hour trying to protect him from any further injury.'

Whereupon I was escorted to a police car and locked in the back. During the time I was there, two people, whom I was later told, were the lad's mother and father, came and looked at me as though I was some sort of monster.

Before being allowed to go I was cautioned on the basis that I could be charged with causing an accident, moving a vehicle (the motorbike) from the scene of the accident and proving a hazard to other road users by parking my car on a slip road leaving a roundabout. I was also given a slip to produce my documents at my nearest police station. While all this went on the police went over my car with a fine tooth comb.

When I got to Tommy's he couldn't believe what had gone on less than five minutes from his front door. I heard about a month later that the police had decided not to prosecute me for anything and that the lad had sustained a broken collarbone. All that for trying to help, a simple thank you would have sufficed.

However we were struggling along, just about finding enough gigs to keep us on the road, when in 1993 Tommy received terrible news. He went into hospital for what, by comparison to what he would be told, was relatively minor surgery on the ulcers which he had been drinking pints of milk to keep at bay, but they were the least of his worries, he was diagnosed with stomach cancer requiring immediate surgery.

This was the start of a very worrying period. Tommy's surgeon Mr Myrick-Thomas said he would perform surgery of the most invasive kind by removing three-quarters of his stomach. 'This,' said Mr Myrick-Thomas, 'should prevent the spread of the cancer.'

Being two hundred miles away up the M1 in Oldham I was not able to be of much support to Tommy and Ida while he was in hospital, although I spoke to Ida on a daily basis. She kept me informed of Tommy's progress and did everything she could to help and support him through his ordeal.

One of the first things I had to do was obtain medical certificates for all the people who had booked Tommy. For the most part the agents expressed concern for his well-being and assured me that as soon as Tommy was fit again he would be rebooked. However, I would be disillusioned by the subsequent actions of certain agents.

The fact that Tommy made such a good recovery and has performed to such a high standard for the last twelve years and hopefully will continue to do so is due to the skill of his consultant. Tommy has often remarked that without this wonderful man he would not be here today.

Tommy was re-booked in all but one case. It would be ten years and even then only after the person who handled the bookings had left the company, before Tommy would work for Warners again. I also suspect that another agent who worked in conjunction with the person in question used the opportunity to address his own agenda and that they colluded in an effort to deprive Tommy of his livelihood. They did not succeed so they are unworthy of having their names mentioned, they know who they are and have found, through other circumstances that what goes around comes around. It is a pity people like this never realise it is the performers who keep them in a job not vice versa.

Tommy and I now have an excellent working relationship with the company through Dave Arnold who is a perfect gentleman and conducts everything in a most professional manner.

Frank Godfrey of the 'Oldies but Goodies' agency booked

Tommy for Butlins Skegness in 2004 and 2005. A very nice comment from the fans was that Tommy Bruce's performance had been worth the admission for the whole week. Sadly Skegness and Bognor are the only two Butlins camps left in England now.

On Tommy's release from hospital, a long convalescence was required, as being the possessor of such a powerful voice the strain on his stomach via his diaphragm is tremendous when he sings. Unfortunately Tommy worried that he might be off the circuit for too long, took a gig from an agent called Robbie Mac, it was to work at a venue that he had worked many times over the years and has great affection for The Lakeside at Frimley Green. I felt it was too soon but he assured me he would be all right. He was in agony from the moment he started to sing, he burst the stitches and the wound bled. Fortunately he managed to get through the performance but it did set his recovery back, it was some time before he was gigging again.

Never one to dwell on the down side of life, Tommy was soon back in the swing of things, so we set about getting his show back on the road. In 1996 Tommy and Ida got married. I was his best man; it was a lovely day and the sound of Tommy's recording of *'Always'* playing in the background during the ceremony set the tone for the day and for the years to come.

Of course on Tommy's wedding day I had to go and make one of my famous mistakes, fortunately this one would not affect

Tommy. Before he and I linked up I had enjoyed a long and reasonably successful sporting career. I had given up playing rugby almost immediately we started on the road together, also I stopped running marathons, as I had little time for training. But rather foolishly I continued to compete in the occasional triathlon, this foolishness would be my downfall. After the wedding I drove up to Manchester with Margaret to catch a flight to Malta the same night. I would be competing in The Malta International Triathlon the following morning. It would turn out to be my last competitive race.

I was not expecting to pull up any trees but I never expected the things that went wrong. In the euphoria that I was feeling about Tommy's wedding I joined Margaret in a few whiskeys on the flight, what a mistake. When we got off the plane I discovered two things; one, my bike was not on the plane and two, the start of the race had been brought forward. I only had an hour to get to the start.

Margaret suggested I pull out but she knew I wouldn't. A friend had found a bike I could borrow so changing on the way I found myself at the start. Flags of all nations fluttering in the breeze, me standing beneath the Union Jack with tears of pride in my country, perhaps fuelled by the whiskey making me feel even more emotional than usual. The gun went and I plunged into the sea, only god knows how many times I was sick, but I eventually came to shore. I leapt on the bike to find it wouldn't change gear and it had no water carrier, I toiled on in the heat of the Malta sun in my own world of pain. As I forced myself, and the bike forward, I could not help but smile because of my own dry sense of humour. I thought to myself there is only one thing on this bike that is well oiled, the rider. Then I thought the only nut that is loose is the one riding it. What the crowds lining the roadside must have been thinking of this obviously escaped lunatic, I will never know but I imagine they laughed for days at the sight of this sun blistered clown smiling to himself although he was clearly in distress.

A New Zealander, whose name I am ashamed to say I don't remember, won the race. I am ashamed because when he finished the race he got straight back on his bike and brought me water, he then stayed near me throughout the run section, as did the coach of the GB team in case I needed more help. This was showing a true spirit of sportsmanship.

I struggled to the end to find the crowd giving me a rapturous reception and the announcer telling my tale of woe. 'Ladies and gentlemen this is Dave Lodge representing Great Britain. He was best man at his friend's wedding in London yesterday, his bike has been lost in transit, he is a vet., well over fifty years old.'

I crossed the line last to find my fellow competitors waiting for me full of praise and encouragement. They all thought I would be back the next year to perform as I had in previous years, I knew it was over, I would never race again. I resolved to put all the energy that I would have expended training and racing, fully behind Tommy.

~*~

We were fortunate at this time to get a gig in Spain that came in two or three times a year which was very handy for Tommy because the flight and accommodation was included as well as the fee so he was able to take Ida with him. In between performances it was like a holiday for them with plenty of time to relax. To do this they would sometimes take a run up the coast to see another old friend who was performing there, Karl Denver. Karl was a great friend to both Tommy and I until his untimely death from a brain tumour.

One great gig came in via Leapy Lee, now resident in Majorca. He was unable to go to the Gambia so he recommended Tommy for the gig. There was no fee as such but Tommy only made one performance and for that he received two return flights, one week's holiday in a first class hotel and a week on safari staying in beautiful lodges. They loved their time there enjoying the beautiful scenery and magnificent animals as they wandered around but Ida found some of the wildlife that joined them in the lodge, like huge spiders and frogs a bit disturbing. She had Tommy running around getting them out and making sure none of them were in their bed before retiring for the night, because of this I do not think the Gambia would be Ida's first choice for a return visit.

Leapy Lee also provided Tommy and Ida with a trip to Majorca when he arranged for Tommy to appear at Santa Ponsa Golf Club. The committee was delighted with Tommy's performance and gave Lee the position of entertainments manager; this meant appearances for his and our friend Jess Conrad.

Tommy appeared at Dagenham Football Social Club in the mid eighties and there was a surprise guest in the audience; Tommy's twin sister Helen, it was a very emotional reunion, they had not seen each other for more than twenty years. Tommy was delighted to see her and gave her his phone number and that of their two other surviving sisters, Connie and Rose. Time passed but none of them heard from her, and Tommy did not have a contact number, it looked as if they had lost touch for good. Then in 2003 I got a phone call from a lady called Patricia Philpot who said her mum was Tommy's sister. She told me her mum was very ill, having just had a serious operation to help her recover from cancer, and she would like to see him. I phoned Tommy, we knew it could only be Helen so contact was made and I took Tommy and his wife Ida to see her. It seemed her whole family was there and although Helen was very weak the joy she felt at being with her brother was very apparent.

As luck would have it Tommy was due to appear at The Wantz

Social Cub nearby very soon, so I arranged for Helen and her family to come and see him. It was a great night and once again an emotional reunion. Even better this time they have stayed in touch.

Dave and Tommy at the opening of the blue plaque to honour Billy Fury

Longevity in pop stars is rare indeed, between Elvis and the Beatles in a time I call 'The Hairspray Music Period' we had Bobby this and Bobby that and few of them really lasted but then Tommy Bruce is a very different kind of star. Indeed Tommy Bruce was an unlikely choice to be a recording star but then the sixties was a time for unlikely success stories. Tommy saw all the changes first hand and this is his story.

Raised in an orphanage Tommy became a household name in Britain because of his rugged good looks and his gravel voice. The boy who went from an orphanage to a garden, to stage and TV fame and fortune. There is only one Tommy Bruce and in this book we really get to know him.

The success of his classic version of *'Ain't Misbehavin'* did more than just establish him as a Columbia recording artiste it gave him a career in television and in the theatres and cabaret lounges the length and breadth of the country. Stars and Garters was only one of the many TV shows that made him a star of the small screen. But it was this show that made him a household name.

Dave Lodge has a unique style and is very observant when it comes to sixties legends. So when the time came for Tommy's official biography to be written there was only one man who could do the job, his friend and manager Dave Lodge. Dave has been with Tommy for years, they have never had a contract just a handshake. Dave is known to just about everyone in the music business as a writer, after dinner speaker and radio broadcaster. He has written this book with real inside knowledge and succeeded in giving us an insight into what it was like to grow up before the big British explosion. He gives a well-balanced account of what life was like for child born in the late thirties right through the forties fifties and sixties and on to the present day.

This account is telling the true story in full, of Tommy Bruce's life for the first time. It is a real page turner and the words leap off every page.

Mike Adams - Author, Broadcaster and Producer.

Chapter Nineteen

As time goes by it seems that the guys who started out in the sixties think of each other when it comes to work. We, whenever a gig comes in, always think 'let's see if we can get Craig, Jess, Wee Willie and the other boys involved in this', and this philosophy is returned by them.

Sadly Heinz died in 2000 and so has been unable to share in many of the good things that have happened for Tommy in recent years. We both miss him very much and mourn the loss of a good friend. We attended his funeral, a very sad occasion with very few of the show business fraternity in attendance. It just goes to show how quickly people forget.

However, one man who was there has since become well-known to us, his name is Tony Harte a performer in his own right who backed Heinz in the seventies. Tony had an idea to promote a show called Rock 'n' Roll Thunder and tour it throughout the UK. In spite of a somewhat erratic approach to life his natural enthusiasm ensured that a friendship came out of the time spent together.

It was decided that Tommy would top the bill, Tony and a

very talented Buddy Holly impersonator called Dave Wickenden would provide support, and incidentally he also became a very good friend. I would be the compère and we would occasionally augment the show with Wee Willie Harris.

This show generated a lot of excitement and interest. As a result it was partly responsible for bringing us back to the attention of Hal Carter. This renewed interest would result in Tommy making an appearance at The London Palladium.

Having just returned from Tommy's on the Saturday morning after gigging the night before, I settled down to watch the rugby on television. I was feeling very tired and relished the idea of a few hours with my feet up. Half watching and dozing I heard the phone ring and for a moment considered letting the answer phone pick up the call, after all it couldn't possibly be anything that wouldn't wait till the following week however, I wearily got up and decided to pick up the phone. When I answered it I heard a very excited Mac Poole asking me if Tommy could be at The Orchard Theatre in Dartford by six-thirty that evening. In the background I could hear Hal Carter so I knew it was going to be a good gig on the Solid Gold Sixties tour. I looked at my watch, twenty minutes to two, yes I said even though I was two hundred miles away.

'Good,' said Hal and Mac, 'because Tommy will be standing in for John Leyton who has a sore throat and if he is still poorly tomorrow Tommy will be needed for The London Palladium.'

I put down the phone and rang Tommy but he wasn't in. I took the snap decision to drive back to Tommy's, as there was no way I would let him miss this gig. I rushed off telling my wife Margaret to keep trying his number and doing the same myself on my mobile (hands free of course), as I drove down.

About half way there Tommy's wife Ida picked up the phone, Tommy's still out she said and not expected back until about six. I refused to admit defeat. Mac kept phoning me on the mobile, I kept reassuring him that there wouldn't be a problem; Tommy would be there.

I pulled up outside his house and ran in, he had not returned. It was now five-forty-five, whilst talking to Ida I began packing his gear, just as I finished Tommy arrived at the front door, a carrier bag in each hand, 'I've been to Sainsbury's,' he said, 'what's happening?'

'Never mind,' I said, pushing him out of the door. 'We are at The Orchard theatre in half an hour and at The Palladium tomorrow.'

We arrived at the Orchard Theatre bang on time much to everyone's surprise. In a blur Tommy changed and went on stage receiving tumultuous applause and a standing ovation at the end of his set.

Collapsing into a chair in the dressing room, Tommy once again asked 'what's happening, how did you get back?'

While I was telling him, Mac Poole came into the dressing room. 'Are you ready for the next one Tommy?' He asked.

'What!' Tommy and I replied.

'Oh, didn't we say,' asked Mac, 'we are doing two shows here tonight?'

The next show was as successful for Tommy as the first. We got the news, from Hal via Mac that Tommy would be needed for The Palladium the next afternoon. The London Palladium is the theatre that Tommy prizes above all others so it was only fitting that he received a standing ovation.

On a sad note I have to say that was the night that Mac told me he was suffering from throat cancer. Tommy and I were deeply shocked and very upset because Mac is an important part of our lives. However showing great courage and resolve Mac took his own path and turned to the Gerson diet as the road to recovery for him and forced the cancer into remission. He is a great man and a great friend.

I have to say that to help him financially another of our friends, Alan Lovell, put on a benefit night for him, and all the boys Tommy, Jess, Danny, Wee Willie, Bruce Welch and Hal Carter to name just a few, all turned out for him. Sheila, Tommy's ex-wife appeared at the Palladium that night with the Vernon Girls and their son Tom and daughter Lorraine along with Tom's partner Lisa and their baby son Bailey were in the audience so it was a very emotional night.

It should never be forgotten how big a part local radio stations have in keeping an artiste's name in the forefront of people's minds. One of the DJs has been so great a help during the past few years that he has become a close personal friend. That man is BBC/GMR presenter Fred Fielder, he helps promote everything that Tommy and I do. Fred first came into our lives a few years ago when I asked him to present Tommy with his gold disc for *'Ain't Misbehavin'*. It had come into my possession as a result of EMI's Manchester Square offices closing down. It had been up on the wall on the stairs leading up to Norrie Paramour's office, along with others presented to artistes like Cliff Richard and Helen Shapiro. I first saw it when we called on business at the offices a few years ago, I was amazed when Tommy told me that that was as close as he had ever been to it, or any of his other presentation discs. I resolved to do everything in my power to ensure as many of them as possible came into his possession. I am pleased to say that the wall of his lounge is now filled with these splendid discs.

Norrie just pointed up to the discs one day saying, 'yours are up there Tom.' Needless to say Tommy, being ever modest and shy, when not performing, was hiding in the other room when Fred tried to make the presentation. I had to literally drag him to the stage as he thought we were all making too much fuss of him.

Of course he is very proud to have it on the wall with his others, as he says, 'that's one more thing to be grateful to his fans for.'

Fred is also well liked and respected by the other sixties guys, in fact he is without doubt one of the most popular men around. Ably assisted by his partner, the lovely and vivacious Arlene he certainly makes the world a better place for all those who know him.

Of course new acts have come along and been incorporated into the show from time to time. People like Jeannie Vincent a great rock and Roll singer with fabulous personality, Dave Wickenden who does a great Buddy Holly show, Dave Chevron with his tribute to Billy Fury also performs a great duo set with his wife Shelly G, they have all certainly enhanced Tommy's shows in recent times.

Tommy is well liked in venues abroad so it continues that he spends a couple of months out of the year in parts of Europe. Always in the company of his wife Ida as they both enjoy their time in the sun.

Tommy and I were invited by Jess Conrad to go along to the unveiling of a blue plaque for Buddy Holly at the only theatre he appeared at in this country. This unveiling would be followed by lunch at The Grosvenor House Hotel in Park Lane. It all sounded a splendid affair and Tommy was looking forward to seeing old friends and possibly meeting new ones. The event was being undertaken by the Heritage Foundation, a charitable organisation who, through its chairman David Graham and show business patrons, raise funds for worthy causes. Unfortunately it was not the most auspicious beginning to what has since become a very friendly association with David and through him the Foundation.

Tommy and I arrived having driven two hundred miles down from Manchester where he had appeared the night before, by-passing Birmingham where he was due to be appearing that night. As soon as he got out of the car he was immediately surrounded by fans who wanted his autograph, never one to refuse to spend time talking with his fans Tommy as always happily obliged. When we eventually reached the entrance to the theatre we were refused admission, as we were not on the guest list. After some discussion I eventually gained entrance for us, but by this time the plaque had already been unveiled by Bruce Welch, rhythm guitarist from The Shadows. I tried to make our presence known to David Graham but he was extremely busy and Tommy's attendance did not register with him.

Making the best of what Tommy felt was a very embarrassing situation I asked Bruce if he would have his photograph taken beside the plaque with Tommy. He readily complied and had a brief but pleasant conversation. We decided to cut our losses and head off to Birmingham where we were appearing that night and forgo the lunch.

I subsequently received a call from Jess Conrad asking why we had not attended the unveiling. My reply was that we had and that Tommy had had his photograph taken with Bruce beside the plaque. I was very upset on Tommy's behalf so I telephoned David Graham on the Monday to express my dismay at Tommy's treatment. His response was just what Tommy and I have since come to expect from the gentleman that he has always proved to be. He apologised and invited Tommy and I to be part of the unveiling of a Blue Plaque for John Lennon at the Old Apple recording studio building, saying that Tommy would be one of the principal guests and treated accordingly.

David, was as good as his word, not only was Tommy made part of the unveiling team but at the lunch later in spite of the day being about John Lennon, Tommy received an award to recognise his having been in show business for more than forty years. Tommy was overwhelmed making a moving speech thanking everyone, saying that his manager and friend Dave Lodge was responsible for this happening, as he was sure he would have left the business by now if 'Dave had not worked so hard to keep the show on the road'.

An amusing little aside to this was Tommy's meeting with Jean Claude van Damme. Jean Claude looked at Tommy's rugged features and said, 'You've got a great face man,' whereupon Jess Conrad, who is undeniably one of the most handsome men in show business, or anywhere else for that matter, piped up tongue-in-cheek 'what about mine?' Jean Claude looked at him for a moment before replying, 'no' there was great hilarity at this with Jess himself leading the laughter.

Tommy was delighted to find that also attending the lunch were old show business pals some of whom he hadn't seen for many years. Harry Fowler being one old mate he was delighted to see again, of course, Harry was greeted in true Tommy fashion with the words, 'Well, if it ain't 'Arry the 'orse.'

Another reunion with Andrew Ray brought great joy to Tommy who related to me just what great mates they had been in the sixties only losing touch when Tommy moved north. They parted company promising not to lose touch again, unfortunately, quite unexpectedly Andy collapsed and died the following week.

Our association with the Heritage has brought Tommy and I a lot of pleasure mixing with old friends like Billie Davis, Kay Garner and Chas Mcdevitt and with new, Jean Ferguson, Vikki Michelle and Philip Madoc. Another great guy who has come back into Tommy's life is Tom O'Connor, we see Tom in various places and at functions like the Heritage lunches and Encore Magazine awards.

One name from the Parnes days who came along and gave Tommy a great gig in Grantham, is Vince Eager. Vince had been working abroad and on cruise ships for some years and on the back of his highly successful Raised on Rock tour he decided to put on a show in his local area for three nights. The local press reported that this was the most exciting show the area had seen for many years.

Always trying to get Tommy's profile lifted led me to get him on Mark Lammar's *Never Mind The Buzzcocks* show. I also managed to get some of the other guys like Craig Douglas, Jess Conrad and Danny Williams on the show. Of course this appearance would not be without its own humour. The purpose of Tommy's appearance on the show would be to see if the panel could identify him from a line up after seeing him perform in a film clip from more than thirty years ago. Joining Tommy in the line up I was given position number one, Tommy position number five. Mark Lammar asked; 'is it number one, the big bruiser', going down the line until he got to Tommy, saying 'or is it number five, the self-abuser'. How we kept our faces straight I will never know but we certainly laughed about it afterwards.

Needless to say the panel guessed right at number five. Tommy then received an ecstatic reception from the television audience, just goes to show class will tell no matter what the introduction. If the people responsible for television entertainment only took the trouble to find out, there is a huge audience out there who would love to see real variety shows on television and be entertained by artistes from their youth.

Many of our contemporaries don't watch television after nine o'clock most evenings as they are not interested in which celebrity is being sick for the camera, or which chef can swear the most. Or even how to turn your house into something you didn't want in the first place.

Incidentally Craig Douglas who has been around for the best part of fifty years is one of the finest entertainers performing today, Tommy has often been found in the wings watching Craig's performance when they are on the same bill. We both feel that Craig is a real gentleman and always enjoy being with him. He has supported us through good times and bad.

Danny Williams is another performer Tommy admires. If anything his wonderful voice appears to have improved with the passing of time. Best remembered for his recording of *'Moon River'* Danny is a consummate performer with a wonderful voice. He has always been a very good friend. *(Since writing Danny has passed away, see later pages)*.

The night Tommy appeared coincided with one of Tony Christie's comeback appearances as part of the Comic Relief promotion of his popular song *'Is This Way to Amarillo'*. Tommy had worked with Tony before and I had known him in his early days when he sang with a band called The Trackers we were pleased to find that time had not changed him, a lovely guy with a great talent. He is now managed by his son Sean another really nice guy we wish them continued success.

Another really friendly man who appeared that night was Bez from the Happy Mondays. Bez, contrary to what publicity would have you believe, is an intelligent, articulate guy with a strong family ethic. Tommy and I enjoyed the time spent in his company.

We continued to gig around the country and I was starting to get worried about Tommy, he was losing weight and not eating. Every time we stopped at the services he bought milk, and when we got close to our destination he would say, 'see if you can find a shop Davey and get a pint of milk for me'.

This was too reminiscent of the eighties and early nineties for my liking, when we could have kept United Dairies in business. I continued to express my concern but Tommy, I think, was in denial at this point and although worried he did not want to accept that something might be wrong.

Things came to a head in May when we did a gig in Eccles on the outskirts of Manchester. Tommy was in a lot of pain with his back and had lost weight again. My wife Margaret expressed her concern to Ida and she agreed that his health was a worry to her.

Of course at this point it should be said we were all worried about Ida, who was having health problems of her own. Thankfully these are now resolved and she is well but obviously under stress because of her love for Tommy and her need to see him fit again.

The show itself was not the best as the guy who booked us

had said that Tommy and the band could use the house PA. One of the best in the north he said, 'so don't let the band bring their own as they might upset the balance.'

I should have known better and told Mac to bring the band's PA, we normally have it in reserve no matter what and I think it shows how worried I was about Tommy's health that I did not ensure its arrival. As it turned out the house PA wasn't suitable for a band, only for use with backing tracks.

Mac and the boys worked extremely hard to cobble something together using their own back line and Tommy sang through the house mike. It sounded remarkably good in the circumstances but not the sound quality we normally like to present. Also Tommy's discomfort with his back pain made me feel worse about the whole thing. Bad enough that he should be subjected to an unprofessional arrangement, but worse still that I was contributing to putting extra pressure on him.

Because I was so worried we went down to see Tommy in early June. To our great distress we found he had lost over a stone in weight since I'd seen him last. Ida was extremely concerned for him, after some discussion the four of us all agreed, he must see the doctor, which he did on the following Monday. The doctor said he would arrange hospital tests to see what the problem was.

Although we were worried we carried on much as before. I

for my part will always carry a burden of guilt that I could not do more to convince my much loved friend, that he needed to seek medical help sooner, I feel that because of me he is suffering much more than he needed to. He would have had much more fighting strength if I could have made my feelings clearer. Thankfully he is a true fighter and I pray he will win this huge battle, with Ida by his side to help him.

As Tommy's sixty-eighth birthday coincided wth his daughter Lorraine's appearance in a play called *'Get Ken Barlow'* at the Coliseum theatre in Watford it was decided we would go and see her. It was a great evening, we met Tommy's son and his wife Lisa there and really enjoyed the play. Lorraine was a tour de force and we had a splendid time.

After the show we all went for a meal together in a little Italian restaurant. It was a wonderful social occasion, pleasant conversation in convivial surroundings. Young Tommy and Lisa had parked in a different place from us, so we said goodnight and agreed to meet for lunch the next day. Lorraine, Tommy and I went back to the car and paid the fee only to be greeted by the words on screen 'machine out of order'. 'Just drive the car up to the barrier Dave,' said Lorraine, 'you've paid your money it might go up'.

I drove towards the barrier with no confidence in her words. It went up all right, but not under its own steam, Lorraine walked forward got hold of the barrier and lifted it into the air like a female version of the Incredible Hulk, I drove through and she lowered it gently into place.

This done she walked over, leaned into the car, kissed me goodnight, having previously kissed her dad before he got in the car, and disappeared into the night. Tommy and I sat in disbelief smiling ruefully and thinking how like two poor old men having to be helped by a bright young lady we appeared. I think you are more inclined to have the confidence to do things like that when you are young, as you get older you tend to see consequences. We would probably have left the car, walked home and gone back the next day.

Shortly after our night out Tommy got word that he had the appointment for his tests, they would be carried out over a period of two weeks. The tests showed the cancer had returned after twelve years. It had affected his stomach, the bones in his back and touched one of his lungs.

Treatment started immediately but he began suffering an adverse reaction to the treatment and had a really hard time of it in the early weeks, finding himself unable to eat and being sick all the time.

His first response was understandable, he felt angry and bitter that this disease should be visited on him again. He is a clean living man who has looked after himself, never abusing his body, following a self- imposed edict of all things in moderation. He was in complete despair and I feared that in spite of Ida's efforts on his behalf he would not rally. However, I should have known better, Tommy is a fighter and he grasped the nettle. He is now showing great resolve and supported by Ida, he is fighting back and looking forward to the future. He fully intends to be back on stage performing his beloved Rock'n' Roll.

It was at this point I decided to attempt something that had been playing on my mind for a couple of years. Tommy's friend, Albert, had made a frame for the original acetate Barry Mason had taken up to Norrie Paramour all those years before. The framed disc had stayed in Mildred's care since Albert's demise and I had often wondered if it would actually play after more than forty-five years. Now seemed a good time to find out.

I took it along to my friend, Dave Robin's, known as Chevvy to his friends, Chevron Music Studios. There, with considerable trepidation, I set about removing the acetate from the frame. Albert's work was like everything else about the man, of the highest quality and the screw back he had made was easily removed. As I carefully passed the acetate to Chevvy I could not help but think that I was holding in my hands something that had changed Tommy's life in an incredible way.

It was apparent immediately that the A-side, *'Ain't Misbehavin'* was certainly unplayable. However the B-side looked as though we might have a chance with it.

Chevvy placed it on the turntable and unbelievably a sound that had not been heard for forty-six years assailed our ears. Through the pops and crackles that time had enhanced Tommy Bruce sang Anthony Newley's hit song *'Why'*. His timing and phrasing were just superb.

With just a simple piano backing he achieved something remarkable, he sounded like a singing star. This was all the more surprising when you consider he had never sung anywhere except in the bath before. No wonder Norrie Paramour recognised in Tommy's voice something that would make him a star.

So as Chevvy applied his technical skills to the task of improving the sound quality, we both pondered on the likelihood of anyone before or since having displayed enough vocal talent on their first attempt at singing, to achieve a recording contract when the person judging them had never even seen them.

It also says a lot about the feel Barry Mason had for music at such an early stage in his career. For my part it confirmed what I had known from the first time I heard Tommy sing, he is that rare breed that very occasionally turns up in all walks of life, a natural. I will never cease in my efforts to bring his talent to a wider audience.

After some considerable time and effort Chevvy produced an excellent CD of the song and I took it down for Tommy to listen to. Having kept my idea a secret from him I knew he would be surprised to hear it, but I was not prepared for how surprised Tommy would be. I put it on his CD player with the words, 'see what you think of this Tom; it's one of the new boys'.

When he heard it he reacted with stunned silence, he looked at me, at the CD player, and back at me in complete disbelief. Incidentally the piano player was Tony Ross and he played a great swing arrangement for Tommy to sing to.

Finally recovering the power of speech Tommy said 'Barry, what, it can't be I don't believe it, how have you done that it's impossible'. Pausing for breath he continued, 'I have never heard that before. I sang it on the day but I never heard it again. I can't thank you enough, wait until Lorraine and Tom hear that.'

I could not have been more pleased, never in my wildest dreams could I have imagined the level of pleasure my actions would bring him. Both Tommy and I have expressed our pleasure and gratitude to Chevvy as it would not have been possible without him. Maybe we will be able to include the song on a future album. I am sure Tommy's fans would love to hear it, so we will have to make it our next project.

Tommy with his cousin Bill

Passport showing that
Tommy Bruce really is his name.

Tommy and Ida's Wedding Day

Thom, Lisa and Bailey

Showbiz 11

Thomas Jnr

Lorraine

I was pleased to be asked by Tommy's manager Dave Lodge to say a few words about him. Although I know that others who knew him for a longer period of time, for example Freddy Cannon who toured with him in the sixties may have more to say about him on a personal level.

Having met Tommy during my time recording with his AR manager Norrie Paramour, I found that I enjoyed his talent and distinctive *Gravel Voice*. I know that he is still enjoying a wonderful career, although he has not performed for a while due to ill health. I wish him good health and the return to the stage his talent deserves. I can do no more than repeat my dedication to him from way back when. All My Best Always, Bobby.

Bobby Vee

I first met Tommy Bruce through his manager Dave Lodge, (the author of this book). Dave had discovered Tommy's Gold Disc when EMI closed Norrie Paramours office in Manchester Square, London. He had thought about when and where he would present it and decided on Tommy's gig at The Patricroft Conservative Club in Eccles, Manchester.

His next thought was who should present the disc and decided that I was the right person for the job. When he contacted me I was delighted, but there was a slight problem I had already been booked for a function on the same evening. However I felt that this was too good an opportunity to be missed. So I told Dave I would find a way to be there, although it would be a flying visit, as I would have to get back to the people who had booked me. I wonder what they would have thought if they had known that while they were eating their buffet, I had slipped away to present one of the sixties most famous performers with a gold disc.

I have been fortunate to spend time in Tommy's company since and I find him to be a very natural down-to-earth kind of guy. There is no edge on him and it is always a pleasure to speak to him. He has richly deserved the success he has had over the years, long may he continue. I have no hesitation in saying that Tommy and Dave are a couple of good old boys.

Fred Fielder
BBC Broadcaster.

Chapter Twenty

I cannot let the close personal friendship that exists between Tommy, me and Craig Douglas go unmentioned. Craig is always there extending the hand of friendship offering to help and just being Craig, a perfect gentleman who gives of himself freely. He is one of the most talented men of his generation, yet with us he's just our mate.

We are receiving tremendous support from Tommy's fellow performers at this time, to the extent that many of them have agreed to appear in a special Gala Concert for him. This concert is to be held at the Williats Centre, Potters Bar and the level of support has been unbelievable, artistes the calibre of Helen Shapiro, Mike Berry, Graham Fenton. Venon Girls, Chris Black, Johnny Pat, Kay Garner renowned the world over for her vocal talents, and Suzie Glover, who sang with the hit recording group The Brotherhood of Man in the seventies. Also John Leyton, Craig Douglas, Jess Conrad, Cliff Bennett, Danny Williams and Dave Sampson have given their services freely.

One of the lovely things that will happen that night is that Barry Mason will sing on the show. Barry is a frustrated performer whose other talents have been more recognised in the business, so our audience may be surprised by his performance. Once again showing that Tommy is a well-loved and respected performer among his peers.

Another wonderful thing that happened is that a very gifted and talented guitar player, Peter Williams made a recording of 'Lavender Blue' as a tribute to Tommy. It is a marvellous recording, Peter's guitar is his voice and when you listen to it, it is almost as if Tommy is singing.

A very strange thing happened to Peter that has never happen before, he played the song first time as though he knew it, yet it is a song that he had not heard before. He says it was as if someone was guiding his hands. Tommy and I were surprised and amazed by the recording and Tommy said he is very flattered by such a fine musician recording a tribute to him.

Tommy's efforts to force the cancer into remission, with the help and support of his wife, family and the doctors at the Mount Vernon Hospital have been incredible. He has turned the weight loss situation around and got back to a weight of 11 stones. This in spite of suffering sickness, ketones in his kidneys, low blood count and anaemia during the treatment so far. His courage in facing this, allied to the support given to him every minute of every day by his wife Ida, is an inspiration to us all.

~*~

I could not write this book without a mention of agents. As in all walks of life there are good and bad examples of these people. John Williams, actor, great guy, and Helen Shapiro's husband, and I are at the time of writing pursuing a particularly obnoxious, if not, dishonest character who titles himself an agent. It is quite unbelievable the depths that some people are prepared to sink to in their efforts to make a living off the back of other people's talents and efforts. Fortunately I am pleased to say that these people have been few and far between.

On this subject is the hurt that was caused to Tommy by his omission from the Hal Carter Memorial concert at the London Palladium in June 2005. He regarded Hal as a friend and is still bewildered that space could not be found for him to sing even one song in order to pay his own homage to the man.

Of course it's all the more upsetting in the light of his current illness that he missed the chance to perform, as it would have been his last show, at least for the foreseeable future. Not that he would want the sympathy vote, he feels he had the credentials to allow him to perform there, a view shared by many of the other artistes who appeared. Also this was an opinion voiced by people in the audience including members of the music media.

Tommy and I attach no blame to Hal's daughter Abby in this, nor do we to any of his family, in fact we have the greatest respect for them as was proved by our action on the night. Tommy and I had taken the decision to have a presentation piece made, it cost a substantial sum of money but we felt it was something that should be done on behalf of all the artistes who knew and had worked with Hal. It had been our intention that Tommy would present it on the night to Abby, but as Tommy was not in the cast I had our friend and drummer Mac Poole do it for us. I know that Abby and her family were very touched and deeply moved by our action, because she told me so.

Craig Douglas should also, in the opinion of many, have been involved that night, but certain people had their own agenda and made sure that neither he nor Tommy were involved. The only people to really suffer in situations of this nature are the general public who buy the tickets. I know that Tommy was out of consideration before the flyers were printed but many people were amazed that he was not on the bill and commented to that effect.

There were radio and television personalities in the audience who thought, and said, that Tommy must have had a previous engagement, as they could see no other reason for his absence.

It was a purely political and selfish act and the people responsible know who they are and should take a long hard look at themselves and their motivation. More to the point, other members of the music industry know who they are and as was commented to me, what goes around comes around.

You may think it cowardly of me not to name them, but I will not sully Tommy's book with their names. Suffice it to say that on his worst day Tommy Bruce is twice the man any of them are. He has risen above their type throughout his career and will continue to do so.

Our thanks go to Mac Poole for his efforts to help Tommy and Craig Douglas perform that night. He has spoken long and loud in their support and it is just one more example of his previously documented friendship. Craig had just finished the last Solid Gold Sixties tour and for that reason, if no other, should have graced the stage at the London Palladium on this auspicious occasion.

Another of the more serious examples of these people's conduct is to set themselves up as having the right to claim royalties on the songs that other people have recorded. Even going so far as to sell all the rights to people, like Tommy's recordings, on what in the business are referred to as non-specific contracts. This means that if they could find hundreds of recording companies worldwide willing to buy, they can sell all those rights over and over again. This has been done to many artistes not just Tommy, but part of my job as his manager is to be aware of and try and put a stop to, these actions and if possible redress the balance.

I am glad to say that I have been fortunate enough to deal with some of the best in the business on Tommy's behalf and I am thankful for the standards they set and the help they have given me along the way.

Just a few of the many who are among the good guys include, Paul Barrett who for me is a giant of the industry, not just physically, he is a lovely genuine man with a warm sense of humour. Garth Kaywood who Tommy considers a friend of long-standing, as do I, and Roy Hastings if only for all the help he gave Tommy in the seventies.

Johnny Mans who looks after business most notably for Sir Norman Wisdom and Max Bygraves, but he has also helped many others along the way. We are privileged to list him among our friends.

Of course the late great Hal Carter whom we have such great respect for who was the epitome of everything that every good agent should stand for, will never be forgotten whilst Tommy and I are around. He was everything that any agent starting up should try to be and if they achieve a quarter of what Hal achieved they will have done well.

Frank Godfrey from the 'Oldies but Goodies' agency has booked Tommy every year for the last three years to appear at Butlins Skegness. He is a smashing guy who we are always pleased to see. Last year he was told by the fans, that Tommy Bruce's performance was worth the admission for the whole week. As Frank books the camp for the week and then lets off the chalets and books the acts, he took that compliment for himself as well as Tommy. We both agree he deserves it.

A couple of guys more than worthy of mention who have come up with gigs for Tommy over the years are Freddy Humpries, known as *Freddy Boy* to his friends, from Chingford, and Ray Forrester from Leeds who puts all his efforts behind fundraising for cancer charities. These are two men who Tommy has a great deal of time for and we both try to support their efforts whenever possible.

A man who is more than just an agent is Garth Kaywood, Garth has been Tommy's friend for forty years and mine for at least thirty, we both have great respect for him and have enjoyed time in his company. Tommy remembers parties and in particular horse rides with Garth, Nelly, Vince Eager and Michael Cox. Including one occasion when Tommy's horse ran away with him much to the enjoyment of the others. Garth is always thought of with great affection.

A man who is not an agent but who always does a lot to help all the guys is the tailor to the stars Neil Crosland. Neil has been with that lovely man Charlie Williams as his friend and manager from the beginning, but more than that and quite apart from making, in our opinion, the best stage-wear in the business, Neil is a great guy who works tirelessly for charity with the help of his lovely wife Maureen and they never let anyone down. Tommy and I think knowing him and Maureen enriches our lives and we are glad to call him our friend. Incidentally Neil came along to Tommy's

Gala Evening with his friend Dave Selley who provided a white Fender Stratocaster guitar to be signed by the cast. The guitar was then auctioned with all the proceeds going to Tommy.

Among the people in the business who Tommy considers to be his friend is the previously mentioned Danny Williams. Danny has a wonderful voice, best remembered by many for his wonderful recording of *'Moon River'*. Although he had many other recordings to his name, like Tommy he is forever associated with one song. He was one of the first people to step forward and offer his services for Tommy's Gala Concert. Shortly after we spoke Danny phoned me again and told me he had suffered a collapsed lung, but that I should not worry because he would be fit in time for the show. Three weeks later he told me that an advanced stage of cancer had been diagnosed in both lungs. We prepared to support him in his struggle and would have done anything to help him. Sadly we have subsequently learned that within a few weeks, he fought and lost his battle against the big C. He knew, I am sure, that Tommy and I gave him all the love and support possible during his difficult time. We will miss his gentle ways and kindness, he has left us with some wonderful memories. It is strange what a high percentage of entertainers suffer from this dreadful disease. It does not of course matter what walk of life we come from because it seems that we are all destined to be touched by this scourge of the age, either directly or indirectly.

The wonderful thing is that this awful illness has given people the opportunity to let Tommy know how much they think of him. I have received cards, letters and emails in there thousands from his fans including those in other counties. They, I am sure, will be glad to know that Tommy is deeply moved by their support.

We had the splendid Gala evening at The Williatts Centre in Potters Bar on Sunday 15th January 2006. This was an opportunity for performers and fans alike to give their support to Tommy and the response and the turnout was tremendous. So many of Tommy's contemporaries from the sixties came and performed and not one of them even looked for expenses never mind a fee. All the backing musicians also gave their services and did their part for Tommy. It was probably the best line up of British artistes that had been seen on stage at one time for many a long year. Not since the Parnes days have there been line-ups like the one we had on this occasion.

The names who came forward in Tommy's time of need included Helen Shapiro, Craig Douglas, John Leyton, Jess Conrad, Mike Berry, whose contribution to the sound for everybody, on what was a difficult night in that area must not be forgotten, Graham Fenton, Wee Willie Harris, The Vernon Girls, Clem Cattinni, Dave Sampson Danny Rivers and Barry Mason There were many others who would have come if not for pressure of work or transport difficulties getting back from abroad, as in the case of Cliff Bennett and Peter Sarstedt.

It was a truly wonderful evening; our musical director was Mac Poole who worked tirelessly not just behind his drums on the night but also in his efforts to get the show on in the first place. I, as compére and stage manager, simply could not have done it without him.

The musicians who turned out for Tommy made an impressive line up in their own right. We had Roger Mckue, Alan Lovel, Tony Hall, Stuart Rees, Dave St James, Pete Oakman who among his many other talents wrote 'A Picture of You' for Joe Brown and Chris Black. There were others but in the excitement of the evening with nothing written down I just cannot remember any more names, and for this I apologise, their contribution was just as great and is much appreciated. The show was opened by Dave and Ann who together form a great duo known as The Chevrons. We were also lucky to have Kay Garner, the lovely Polly Raymond and Suzie Glover as backing singers. Polly sang with The Tornados and there was a guest appearance from Johnny Pat a singer from Hull who raised more than a £100 for Tommy in sponsorship.

It should be mentioned that as our great friend Danny Williams had died prior to the show and as he was one of the first to volunteer to perform, we really wanted him to play a part in the evening. After some discussion with his son Anthony, daughter Natalie and his manager Elliott Brooks it was decided to show a DVD from

Danny's personal collection of him singing, *'Dancing Easy'* and of course *'Moon River'* backed by Henry Mancini. I am pleased to say that this showing brought the house down. So allowing Danny's wish to help Tommy to be fulfilled and also to provide a fitting tribute to Danny himself.

For me the highlight of a great evening was the standing ovation given to Tommy by the whole audience and the cast of the show. It was a wonderful feeling for all concern to know that we had succeeded in putting on a memorable evening. Just to put the icing on the cake, the show was captured on film by Mac's two hard-working sons, Matthew and Jonathan. We were also very lucky to have the catering skills back stage of Mac's wife Maria and my wife Margaret. A great team effort for Tommy.

was plenty of rock support at the christening at Woodford on Sunday of BERENICE COOPER
d after Berenice Kinn, wife of the NME managing director, Maurice Kinn, who are both now in
lia), seen in the arms of god-father JOE BROWN, with the parents GEORGE and DORIS COOPER
h side. Others at the happy event were (l to r) JOHNNY KIDD, VINCE EAGER, PETER FLEE-
REKKER, MARTY WILDE, MIKE PRESTON and TOMMY BRUCE.

All the Band Leaders

Helen Shapiro

Ruby Murray and her
husband with Tommy

Peggy Lee

Tommy Bruce and Miss Billie Davis
With
THE BRUISERS

Special guests

BLUE'S n TWO'S

poster for a tour that
was scheduled but didnt
go ahead because of
illness

America has Louis Armstrong and we had Tommy Bruce; well, Tommy's voice wasn't as gravely as the great Sachmo's, but it had a deep, velvet richness about it.

It was unmistakable when it came over the airwaves and Tommy could do his own take on classics like *'Lavender Blue'* and *'Ain't Misbehavin''* and do it with a twinkle in his eye. He would give an element of humour to the songs, which meant that Tommy had a head start in the comic stakes.

In the great series *'Stars & Garters'* which brought the homespun warmth of a cockney sing-a-long pub into the living rooms of the nation, Tommy was in his element with his great deep-throated cockney accent. If you put him into different situations he'd be guaranteed to give you a laugh.

But Tommy settled up north and it's funny that a town or a city can become synonymous with an individual and anytime anyone would mention Warrington it was swiftly followed by a 'Ah Tommy Bruce'. Although he has now moved, Tommy had made his home there for a long time and his family made great friends with the locals - Friends of the family to this day.

There's always a smile from Tommy, always an hello and that's why he still survives in this ever-changing industry of show business because he is always there. If there is a big nostalgia event everybody's on the phone to book Tommy because he helps us relive our teenage memories.

The Golden age of the sixties music was noted for its great songs filled with melodic structure and meaningful lyrics, but it was also noted for its diversity and Tommy enriched that diversity with his instantly recognisable voice; you knew the second you heard it that that voice could only belong to one person - Tommy Bruce.

Jimmy Cricket

Award for over 45 years in showbiz

Barry Mason, Harry Fowler and Tommy

Chapter Twenty One

I write this part of the story not for the first time with tears in my eyes as today the 8th of February 2006 I have received the wonderful news that Tommy's specialist has given him the all clear. Obviously he is going to need regular check ups and he will need to take care of himself, but the word euphoric is the only one to describe how I feel at this wonderful news.

By the time this book comes to publication Tommy will have received a Heritage Foundation award in recognition of his outstanding contribution to entertainment over a period of almost fifty years. The chairman David Graham, Annual President Rick Wakeman, the directors and all those involved with the foundation are adamant in their view that he is more than worthy of this award. Indeed they would have presented it to him last year if he had been well enough to attend a presentation lunch.

Tommy is determined to perform again if only so that he can thank all the many people who have supported him through these difficult days. As so many of them have said, 'the best thanks they can have is to see him out there on stage again doing what he does best'.

All Tommy's fans are wonderful but a couple of them are worthy of special mention. Pat and Ken Hellier are no longer with us, both having died in the last couple of years, but their kindness and support over many years was incredible. Everywhere we appeared you could count on Pat and Ken's smiling faces being in the crowd, Tommy and I miss them terribly and will not forget them.

I for my part feel blessed to know and have this man as he says, 'as my brother'. I want our relationship to continue for many years to come, as I feel the pleasures in store are as great as those that have gone before. There are definitely more days to be spent in the pie and mash shop.

Tommy Bruce is a fabulous entertainer; his collection of Platinum, Gold and Silver discs is second to none. They are a testament to the record buying public's affection for him and his wonderful voice. His countless standing ovations in theatres up and down the country continue to this very day.

He is in my opinion among the very best of British entertainers, the undisputed master of his craft. The unique and very special international singing and recording star:

The Man with The Gravel Voice:

Mr Tommy Bruce!

Postscript

Once again I am reminded of the generosity and friendship of Tommy's contemporaries. Several of the great artistes from the early days of the Merseybeat scene got together at Huyton Conservative Club to perform in benefit for Tommy. It was organized by Karl Terry and he put a tremendous amount of work into a great night.

Those who were in attendance and performed that night included Karl himself with his band The Cruisers, Decca recording star Lee Curtis, who had a number 1 hit in Germany with *Let's Stomp*. Kingsize Teddy Taylor who recorded the great song *Stupidity* and is widely credited with being the man who taught The Beatles how it should be done. Geoff Nugent with The Undertakers another great performer and band of the sixties who enjoyed success on the Pye label with songs like *Money* and *Just A Little Bit*. Nicky Crouch and his Mojos Nicky also performed with Faron's Flamingos. Last but by no means least Jason Eddie aka Albie Wycherly, Billy Fury's brother who as previously stated has been a life-long friend of Tommy's.

All of these artistes achieved legendary status in Germany where they appeared at The Star Club and other venues and are still in great demand over there today. The fact that they gave freely of their time on Tommy's behalf speaks volumes for the impression Tommy has made on performers everywhere over the years.

Once again we also have to thank all the many fans who turned out to support the artistes and Tommy. It shows once again the bond that can only be described as love that exists between Tommy and his audience. It is as if they didn't just buy his records they became a part of his life.

Discography

Singles

Ain't misbehavin' Got the water boiling	Columbia DB4453	1960
I'm on fire Broken doll	Columbia DB4498	1960
My little girl On the sunny side of the street	Columbia DB4532	1960
I'm crazy about my baby You make love so well	Columbia DB4581	1960
Love honour & oh baby I'm going to sit right down & write myself a letter	Columbia DB4682	1962
Babbette Honey girl you're lonely	Columbia DB4776	1962
Horror movies It's you	Columbia DB4850	1962
Buttons & bows London boys	Columbia DB4927	1963
Lets do it Two left feet	Columbia DB7025	1963
Lavender blue Sixteen years ago tonight	Columbia DB7132	1963
Let it be me No more	Columbia DB7241	1964
Over suzanne It's driving me wild	Columbia DB7387	1964
Boom boom Can your monkey do the dog	Polydor DN 56006	1965
Monster gonzales It' hard getting up in the morning	RCA 1535	1966
I've Been Around Too Long Where The Colour Of The Soil Is Different	CBS 3405	1968
Heartbreak Melody The Reason Why	CBS 3937	1968

mmy Bruce & The Bruisers - knockout	Columbia Seg 8077	1960
mmy Bruce & The Bruisers	EMI Nut EP series 2303	1970

arious Artistes Saturday Club Tommy Bruce	Parlophone PMCII30	1960
n the Sunny Side of the Street arious Artistes Live at The Stars & Garters Club		1968-70
ommy Bruce –The Hits	Autograph	1985
n On Fire	Teenager	1991

ommy Bruce – The London Boy	DAL1	2000
ommy Bruce & The Bruisers that's Rock 'n' Roll	RPM241	2002
he Definitive Tommy Bruce Collection	DAL2	2005

The author of this book Dave Lodge, although now retired from 'the business' is happy to do talks about his time on the road with Tommy Bruce and his fellow artistes.

If you are a club, organisation or charity looking for an interesting talk about what it was like 'doing the rounds' with some of the biggest stars from the 1960s please get in touch for more details.

Dave Lodge can be contacted via email at:
florrieandfred@btinternet.com
or via phone on:
07946 442 604

Pixel✖tweaks
PUBLICATIONS
ULVERSTON · CUMBRIA

LOOKING TO GET
YOUR BOOK IN PRINT?

When faced with publishing your book it can seem that writing it was the easy part. Not only must you now wrestle with formatting text and adding pictures, you need to understand publishing jargon & get it printed and distributed too!

THIS IS THE PART WHERE WE COME IN

Pixel Tweaks Publications takes the pain out of self publishing

We produce a professional looking book from your manuscript including cover design. We offer a print-on-demand service ... which means you can order any quantity of books to distribute to local book shops, plus it will go onto online stores such as Amazon. All at an affordable price then you'll soon recoup your initial costs and begin to make money from your creation!

WANT MORE INFORMATION?
CONTACT US TODAY FOR A NO OBLIGATION CHAT

Tel: Ulverston 01229 343658 • Email: info@pixeltweaks.co.uk

WWW.PIXELTWEAKSPUBLICATIONS.COM

Lightning Source UK Ltd.
Milton Keynes UK
UKHW020605240519
343218UK00007B/669/P